MW00929699

PREFACE

The ballot box successes that the Democrats experienced in 2006 and 2008 came to a stark end with the midterm elections of 2010 when the Republicans won 63 new seats in the House of Representatives and control of that chamber. The Democrats also lost seven Senate seats as well. As I wrote a year ago, in February 2010, the Democrats in the White House and on Capitol Hill were in trouble. General opinion across the United States was that the Obama administration spent too much time and political capital in its first year on health care reform while the unemployment rate continued at nearly 10%. President Obama promised transparency in government after eight years of the George W. Bush administration during which time a great deal of national policy decision-making, including decisions about the federal budget, was made behind closed doors at the White House. But by November of 2010, when millions of Americans had lost their jobs, their retirement plans, and their homes when Wall Street seemed to have survived yet again, many turned to the Republican backed tea party candidates who promised to cut the size of government and taxes as well.

But let us recall that President Obama inherited the worst combined economic recession and fiscal crises since the 1930s. On February 17, 2009, he signed in to law a stimulus package of $787 billion passed by Congress with very little Republican support on Capitol Hill. (This was in addition to the $700 billion bill that Congress passed in the fall of 2008 and President George W. Bush signed in to law to aid the failing financial institutions of the country.) This effort to stimulate the American economy was the largest funding bill ever passed by Congress. It was an effort to put millions of people back to work and to save millions of other jobs. To indicate the reality of the promise of transparency in government, the Obama White House established www.recovery.gov for anyone with access to the internet to track the spending, state by state, of this huge amount of money. Despite these efforts by Washington, the unemployment rate in the United States remained high after nearly two years of the Obama presidency.

Much changed in Washington, and in the country as a whole, after the attacks of September 11, 2001. The costs of the wars in Afghanistan and Iraq have grown to over $800 billion and paying for heightened Homeland Security has grown annually. These commitments to the national and homeland security have meant an increase in annual federal government expenditures at a cost of those budgets of the federal domestic agencies such as the Bureau of Land Management, the Department of Transportation, and the federal judiciary. It is important to remember that prior to September 11, the economy was in a recession and that President George W. Bush's promised tax cut had been passed by Congress and signed into law in the spring of 2001. Both of these actions seem to have contributed to the end of surpluses and the return of deficit spending. Setting priorities for spending in a time of war on terrorism, wars in Iraq and Afghanistan, hurricane catastrophes, and increasing social spending for the elderly have returned to the budget debate between Capitol Hill and the White House.

In the summer of 2011, the Congress and the White House struggled with increasing the debt limit of the United States. As a result of the agreement to raise the ceiling to prevent the U.S. government from defaulting, a congressional Supercommittee was created to find at least $1.2 trillion in savings over the next ten years. Because of a disagreement between raising taxes, supported by the Democrats and not supported by the Republicans, and proposed cuts to entitlements, supported by the Republicans and not supported by the Democrats, the committee failed to address the long term problems of government spending and deficit spending. The result of the Supercommittee's failure will potentially trigger automatic cuts to federal spending of $1.2 trillion across the board to be enacted in FY 2013.

The Power of the Purse contains very basic information on how the budget process unfolds each year in Washington and how you as a citizen can play a part. The more you know and understand the process, the more you can make your lawmakers accountable for your tax dollars. How a nation spends its money says a great deal about its values as a culture and a society. This book is meant to be a layperson's guide to the budget discussion in Washington. Whether you are a U.S. citizen, a student, a foreign diplomat, a businessman, a lobbyist, or any other interested party, you will find this manual both informative and useful.

I have been teaching seminars and studying the federal government in Washington for 30 years. My classes have taken place not only Washington, but also across the country. In that time, I have seen many changes in peoples' attitudes toward government, both here in the capital and in states and localities. Cynicism of government at all levels seems to permeate the American society. Of great concern to me is this lack of appreciation for the only country in the world that has ever tried to do so much for so many all at the same time. Our form of government is that of a republic. The word republic comes from Latin and Greek words that mean "the people", hence the opening line of the U.S. Constitution, "We the people...". Such a notion suggests that care and cultivation of the republic by all of us is a responsibility to keep it alive, growing, and evolving. Perhaps, we have been ripping at the republic because of just what we want or lack, rather than nurturing it by having the same sense of community that built this country. Our new President began his involvement in public life as a community organizer. That he continues to think and to act, as President, as our national leader, with the needs of American community has been questioned in recent days. The battle over budget for 2012 has begun.

But no matter who is president, responsible citizenship suggests an informed people who make their elected officials accountable for the spending of the public's money. Disinterest, perhaps, has contributed to cynicism. Disinterest by the people will not make the elected officials accountable. By not only reading, but using The Power of the Purse, I hope that you will start to feel an ownership in the federal government. After all, it is yours.

Patricia D. Woods, Ph.D.
President
Woods Institute

CONTENTS

1 | THE HISTORIC STRUGGLE OVER THE POWER OF THE PURSE

Most American citizens do not realize how short the history of the United States government is. The governments and economies of current-day Asia and Europe evolved over many centuries and even thousands of years. America's story is only about 240 years old. It begins in the 1770s during the Revolutionary War. The pages that follow will not be too lengthy for you to read, but they will present the context for the thinking about money and taxes over time that is important to appreciating the system in the United States in the 21st century.

A basic review of history also will provide insight into citizens' attitudes toward government today. With the exception of Native Americans and African Americans, most people who settled in the English colonies in the 17th and 18th centuries crossed the Atlantic Ocean to North America to "get the government off their backs." Familiar phrase isn't it? Some came for religious freedom from the state-run Anglican Church that existed in England. Remember the Pilgrims in New England, the Quakers in

Pennsylvania, and the Methodists in Georgia? These people, along with thousands of others in Europe, were tired of the kings' and lords' control over their lives and property whether through royal ownership or the heavy burden of taxation.   They wanted to be on their own, to be free from any king's or government's interference. They desired to be independent. Keep this in mind as we begin.

Eighteenth Century Beginnings

One of the few slogans in our country's history that Americans who have studied its past remember is "no taxation without representation." This rallying cry provided a banner of sorts during the American Revolution when the colonists felt that the British Parliament was taxing them unfairly. Remember the Boston Tea Party? The colonists who dumped tea into the Boston Harbor in 1774 spoke for many people in the 13 colonies who were not happy about the tea tax that the English had levied.   With no political representation in the British parliament, the colonies believed that such taxes on imported tea, glass, lead, and paint were unfair.

Independence from England was declared in 1776, and the Revolutionary war was won in 1783. The Articles of Confederation - the first Constitution - framed the first U.S. Government.   Fearful of too strong a central government similar to Parliament and the King, the authors of the Articles provided for a loose federation of 13 states in which most of the governing power over people's lives was invested. There was no national treasury to issue national currency. Each state levied taxes and tariffs in different ways. Improved land (farm land) proved to be a major source of tax revenue.

Farmers in western Massachusetts reacted quite forcefully to land taxes. Once again, money and taxation played a role in 1786 when Daniel Shays of Massachusetts and his farming neighbors rebelled against the taxes that the legislature was passing to pay for the state's debts incurred during the Revolutionary War. Feeling that the wealthy bondholders of the debt were making out like bandits, Shays and his band of farmers rose up against the state's government in the fall of 1786, but were put

Commonwealth of Massachusetts.

By His Excellency

JAMES BOWDOIN, *Esquire,*

Governour of the Commonwealth of Massachusetts.

AN ADDRESS,

To the good People of the Commonwealth.

[Published by Authority.]

down by January. Eventually pardoned and released from prison, Shays did manage to gain tax relief for his fellow citizens of western Massachusetts. This failed uprising led to the calling of the Constitutional Convention in Philadelphia in the late spring of 1787.

The people who met in Philadelphia did not trust human nature in terms of power and greed, and balked at putting too much power in any one place in the national government because of their experience with Parliament and the Crown. They set up a system of government with three parts - the executive, the legislative, and the judiciary - each of which could stop the action of the other.

It should also be pointed out that in the 18th century, the common people - people like Daniel Shays, people like ourselves - were referred to by the landed gentry, the wealthy shippers, and merchants as "the vulgar herd." The men who met in Philadelphia from May until September 1787 (behind closed doors) represented that propertied group of people. But they were smart enough to realize that the "herd" or most of the people did not need them, the few. They realized that they needed the many or "the people" to support the national government. They were convinced that they needed a hook to make "the people" feel a part of the national government. It should be noted here that in their minds "the people" consisted of white males who owned a certain amount of property. Women and African Americans - who were most of the adult population in the United States at the time - were excluded. But Shays and his small farmer friends had given an only too-real example of the feelings and potential actions of the common person.

Article I of the Constitution actually outlines the powers of the legislative branch, not the executive branch. A description of the House of Representatives and who can run for it precedes discussion of the Senate. This was all rather clever on their part. One of the longest debates that took place during the Constitutional Convention was over what name to give the part of the new national government that the people would feel closest to. Not the House of Commons or Statesmen or Delegates. These were dismissed. The House of Representatives provided the connection with the revolutionary slogan over taxes. As they drafted Article I, which outlines the powers of Congress, they placed in Section 7 the language "All Bills for raising Revenue (taxes) shall originate in the House of Representatives." Direct election of members to this house of Congress by the people has taken place from the first Congress. The term then, as it is now, was for two years, with the idea being that if you didn't like the way they were "taking your money" or taxing you, you had the right to throw them out in the polling booth on election day every two years.

Even though there was direct election of the members of the House of Representatives, the Founding Fathers in Philadelphia still did not fully trust the people. Thus, they created the U.S. Senate to be indirectly elected by the state legislatures. It took a constitutional amendment in 1913, the Seventeenth Amendment, for there to be direct election of U.S. senators by the people. To remove even more political power from the people, they created the electoral college to elect the President. This institution has also changed in the twentieth century.

But no matter how removed these other offices were from election by the people, when the Constitution was finally ratified by the required nine states in the early summer of 1788, the power of the purse - the power of the federal, national government to tax the citizens of the United States of America - rested in the House of Representatives, the people's house, for the first time ever.

Indication of just where this power rested became quite clear during the very first Congress that took place in the spring in 1789 following George Washington's inauguration in New York City. The new Secretary of the Treasury, Alexander Hamilton, came into the House of Representatives just a few days after it had begun to deliberate to announce that there was no money

in the treasury. He offered up his list of ideas for taxes and tariffs that, if passed by the House, would make the struggling young republic solvent. At least he came to the right place but was thrown out when members reminded him that under the Constitution taxes were to originate in House of Representatives and not in the Treasury Department of the executive branch. The precedent was thus set from the very first Congress as to power over the people's money by the people's elected representatives. So important was this issue of taxes to the members of the first House of Representatives that they established the Committee on Ways and Means, the tax committee, which today is the oldest standing committee in the U.S. Congress.

The Early National Period

The first three decades in the nineteenth century are often referred to by American historians as the Early National Period, those years in which the young republic began to grow from essentially a farming country to more of a manufacturing and industrial one. In these years, much of the initiative for doing the business of the federal government came from Congress. As the country began to grow, the bridges, roads, canals, and first railroads became necessary to push back the frontier. Known as "internal improvements," these undertakings were largely funded by Congress which voted the taxes necessary to encourage domestic growth. They also voted the tariffs that citizens needed to protect their struggling factories and businesses from manufactured goods from Europe.

In the realm of foreign policy, Congress, led by Henry Clay of Kentucky and his "War Hawks" of the rising New West, declared war on Great Britain. The War of 1812 was waged in an effort to secure the continent by securing control of the Mississippi River. Victorious in the war, Americans began to push even further west to fulfill the Manifest Destiny to "take the whole continent."

The Andrew Jackson Presidency

Andrew Jackson, known by many in his day as "Old Hickory," served as President from 1829-1836. Being from Tennessee, he was the first president to be elected from a state west of the Appalachian Mountains, breaking the hold on the White House of Virginia and Massachusetts. Seeing himself to be a "man of the people," he asserted the executive power of the Presidency as none of his predecessors had. During his years in the

White House, he managed to terminate the National Bank, take on the tariff question, and to even take on Congress itself when he vetoed many of their bills. Often called "King Andrew" by many of his critics on Capitol Hill, his actions were precursors to much of the executive authority that is exercised by modern presidents.

The Civil War Years to 1921

It was during the Civil War years that the President began to take a more pro-active role in the money process for running the federal government. Abraham Lincoln desperately needed funds from Congress to support the war to save the Union. For the most part, Congress gave him what he needed. Indeed, during the war years, appropriations committees became permanent committees in Congress.

With the Union preserved, the status and stature of the President of the United States began to change both internationally and domestically between 1865 and 1920. It should be noted that in the late nineteenth century, the world's superpower was Great Britain with its vast worldwide empire. It was not the United States. But over this 55-year period, our country did emerge as a major world player.

Internationally, the President's role as commander in chief was enhanced on the world stage. Remember the Maine? It was the American ship that blew up in the Havana harbor in 1898, the event which prompted our war with Spain, an Old World Power. The young, emerging nation-state of the United States of America defeated Spain, acquiring the Philippines and other possessions in the Spanish empire. We were emerging as a power on the international scene. And who was our commander in chief? The President of the United States. In 1917, the United States went to war in Europe and emerged victorious. Although Woodrow Wilson could not convince the Senate to consent to the Treaty of Versailles, he, as commander in chief, led us to victory in World War I.

Domestically during these five decades, the President's stature as chief executive also grew. Following the Civil War, there was much corruption in Washington during the years when U.S. Grant was president, 1869-1876. Much of the problem had to do with nepotism, political payoffs by means of federal employment. Other scandals involving public officials unfolded such that the public began to demand reform. In 1883, the Pendleton Civil Service Reform Act was signed by President Chester A. Arthur. It required examinations to be taken and passed in order to secure employment in the federal government. Professionalism in public service - professionalism of those who worked in the bureaucracy to serve the

President - was now required.

As the country matured, so did the size of the federal government. Departments were created such as Commerce and agencies such as the USDA Forest Service and the Bureau of Reclamation in the Department of the Interior in addition to the regulatory agencies of the Interstate Commerce Commission and the Food and Drug Administration.

Presidents emerged who became more proactive in the legislative process. The first was Republican Theodore Roosevelt who sent to Congress a legislative program called the Square Deal. He had plans to bust the trusts of the robber barons of American capitalism who had exploited poor immigrants, women, and children in their factories  and sweatshops across the country. He skillfully managed to obtain legislation that would regulate the railroads whose lack of price regulation was gouging farmers from the Midwest to the Northwest. With the establishment of the National Forest System, the precedent was set for the federal government's control of public lands for the purposes of conservation. Congress, controlled by the Republicans, gave him a great deal of what he wanted.

But it was Woodrow Wilson who remembered his American history. On the day he was inaugurated in 1913, he called a special session of Congress to whom he personally presented his legislative program, called the New Freedom. He was the first President since John Adams to appear before a joint session of Congress. His programs contained more of the reforms asked for by the Progressive Era in America, reforms that would mean more of a federal government role in the American people's lives. The banking monopoly ended with the establishment of the Federal Reserve System. The creation of the Federal Trade Commission led to the regulation of unfair methods of competition, such as price discrimination and exclusive contracts. The Seamen's Bill improved the safety regulations for seamen as well as their contract negotiating status. And the Democratic-controlled Congress gave him largely what he wanted. Wilson was making the office of the President a more pro-active player in the legislative process. He was not only proposing legislative programs that would cost money, but now he would take them personally to Congress.

The Emergence of the Modern Presidency

Following World War I, it became clear to all that the role of the United States in the world promised to be a great one. The professional career civil service had performed terrifically for the war effort. In 1921, Congress passed the Budget and Accounting Act. This act created a budget office, the Bureau of the Budget, for the President. Before this time, there was no single budget request sent to Capitol Hill by the executive branch for congressional consideration as there is today. Every cabinet secretary and agency head went separately to ask for money. But now with the Bureau of the Budget and with the support of a career professional bureaucracy, the President would send a single budget request for funding for the executive branch to Congress every January for it to consider, appropriate the money for, and pass by July 1, the start of the new fiscal year.

After we roared through the 1920s and crashed in 1929, the American people elected Franklin D. Roosevelt, a Democrat, in 1933 at the depths of the Great Depression. On his inauguration day of March 3, 1933, 26 percent of the employable people in the country were

out of a job. All of the banks were closed. It was a desperate time indeed, but Roosevelt had a plan. Shortly after his term began, he returned to the Democratic-controlled Congress and presented his legislative agenda, the New Deal. The era of the Depression and the New Deal would dramatically change the people's relationship with their federal government.

Every President since FDR has been measured by what he has done during the first 100 days of office, so sweeping were the changes that the New Deal legislation brought across the country. There was no longer the attitude of "get government off my back," but rather "I need a job," and that is what Roosevelt set out to do. Many government agencies were created whose purposes ranged from giving people a job to aid for struggling farmers to improvement of rural life across America. Often referred to as "the alphabet soup programs," the WPA (Works Progress Administration), the CCC (Civilian Conservation Corps), the AAA (Agricultural Adjustment Administration), the REA (Rural Electrification Association), and the TVA (Tennessee Valley Authority) touched the lives of millions of Americans. Whether it was a job or electric power or agricultural price supports, their federal government, not the marketplace of American capitalism, came to the aid of many, many people for the very first time.

It should also be recalled that Social Security

was also passed during this New Deal era. One of the most indigent segments of the American population at that time were the elderly. Many had lost all of their savings in these hard economic times. Many didn't have enough to live on when they no longer worked. Intended initially as a supplement to one's income at the age of 65, the passage of Social Security was the first time that the government would help to "secure" you in your old age. In addition to the elderly, the act also provided for unemployment insurance, aid for the blind and the crippled, and assistance for dependent mothers and their children. This social help from the federal government changed the relationship between the American people and Washington for the future.

From Eisenhower to Nixon: 1950s to 1970s

The United States emerged victorious from World War II as the world's leading nation both militarily and economically. Eisenhower was president and everybody liked Ike. We were the leaders of the free world, armed mightily to defend and to fight, if necessary, in the face of the communist threat of the Soviet Union.

We not only had the bomb, we also had the bucks for as a nation we were unchallenged economically. Our industrial base had not been destroyed by the war. Indeed, most of the industrialized countries of the world had suffered terrible manufacturing infrastructure loss because of the war.

As much as the faces of war-torn Europe and Asia changed so too did domestic life in America. Affluent, prosperous consumer America came into its own during the decade known as "the Fabulous Fifties." Inflation was low; oil was cheap. Unable to buy anything because of the Depression of the 1930s and the war of the 1940s, Americans began to enjoy the good times and to go shopping with a vengeance. There were more consumer goods than ever as well as the resources to purchase them.

When the GIs returned from the war they returned to opportunities that had not existed for most Americans before 1940. They returned to the GI bill, legislation that enabled millions of veterans to go to college for the first time, which would mean a better paying job. They came home to veterans loan programs that made it possible to buy a house for the first time. They began to have babies with many of the women who had left home to work to support the war effort and now returned home. Always on the move (we are a nation of immigrants), there were thousands of young men from farms, ranches, and large cities who had never left home before and had fought in the Pacific or in Europe and had returned safely. They saw that it was indeed possible to leave Dad and Mom, grandparents and relatives, to be thousands of miles away and live a life without the family.

Also in these post-war years, one of the greatest internal American migrations took place when over 7 million African Americans left their homes in the South to find work in the North. Many blacks had served in the military during the war and had performed well, leading to a greater confidence in terms of work and education.

Throughout this decade, Congress continued to give Eisenhower what he asked for largely because of the Cold War. Even though the Democrats controlled Congress for six of the eight years of his presidency, the consensus to wage and win the Cold War united politicians to follow the former leader of the Allied Forces in Europe.

When John F. Kennedy was elected president, the optimism and enthusiasm that the young president brought to the job energized the presidency. A new generation was ready to lead. Kennedy presented

his New Frontier program for changes and reform to a Democratic Congress. Urging programs such as health care for the elderly, federal aid to education, conservation and natural resources preservation, and housing and community development, the young administration's proposals in the domestic area fell on deaf ears in Congress. It was true that much of the nation was prospering. But it was also true that the Congress was in the control of baron-like Democratic committee chairmen, largely from the South, who opposed much of the proposed legislation. Kennedy pressured the House to add members to its Rules Committee so that the power of its chairman, Virginian Howard W. Smith, was somewhat diminished, but he was never able to obtain passage in the House of health coverage for the elderly or federal education aid.

The climate on Capitol Hill changed after the assassination of the young president in November of 1963. Although Kennedy had been a member of Congress, both as a representative and as a senator, he had never been an inside player on Capitol Hill who met behind closed doors in the smoke-filled rooms to cut deals. Thus as president, he had little to trade with his former colleagues on Capitol Hill. However, his successor, Lyndon B. Johnson of Texas, as majority leader of the Senate in the 1950s, not only knew

the environment and had the friends, but had also orchestrated much of the political maneuvering in those years of leadership.

Having large Democratic majorities in both the House and the Senate in addition to the friends from his days as Senate majority leader in the 1950s, Lyndon Johnson succeeded in obtaining funds not only for the War in Vietnam but also for his domestic legislative program, the Great Society. He had known the baronial committee chairmen for years and was able to broker deals with them to obtain passage of dollars for both "guns and butter." The stalled program for health care for the elderly, today known as Medicare, achieved successful passage by Congress as did Medicaid, the health care program for the poor.

Those unsuccessful housing programs for the poor that Kennedy had proposed also saw the light of day and with their passage came a new cabinet post and department, HUD or Housing and Urban Development. Waging a war on poverty, Congress, at the administration's suggestion and insistence, also authorized and appropriated dollars for the Food Stamp program, Head Start, VISTA (the domestic Peace Corps for the poor of Appalachia), and Job Corps (to provide training and remedial education for the poor and dropouts). To qualify for assistance for many of these new programs, an individual had to meet the programmatic criteria set in place by a formula in the law. For example, when an individual reached the age of 65 or was declared permanently disabled before that age, that person would be entitled to Medicare benefits, the heath care program for the elderly. LBJ proposed, and Congress delivered with, the legislation and the money. Party discipline was great in those days of the 1960s. When freshmen members arrived in Congress in those years, they heard from the top "to get along, you go along" with the leadership of your political party.

Paralleling this legislative effort, some would say the cause behind it, was the passage of the Civil Rights Act of 1964, the Voting Rights Act of 1965, the Civil Rights Movement, and the rioting of African Americans in the ghettos of the nation's largest cities. There was a growing awareness by the American people and their political representatives in Washington of the terrible impoverished state of many of those who lived in America's inner cities, most of whom were black.

When Johnson chose not to run because of the escalation of the War in Vietnam, the American people elected Richard Nixon who promised to end the war and wanted to "get government out of Washington." It was in the Nixon years that block grants to states and local governments were created in an effort to return decision-making in government to the entities "closest to the people." Thus, Great Society efforts evolved into the Comprehensive Employment Training Act (CETA), a block grant program to state and local governments offering job training and skills development to the poor. Others included the Community Development Block Grant Program (CDBG) and revenue sharing for state and local governments.

In areas of domestic policy as well as for the war in Southeast Asia, Congress continued to give the President what he wanted. Congress and President Nixon also agreed to index the cost of living allowance (COLA) to the rate of annual inflation for all federal retirement  programs - Social Security, civil service, and veterans programs being the largest. Nixon had a budget office (now called the Office of Management and Budget), professional career civil servants, the best trained military leadership in the world, and better sources of information for budget and policy formulation than the legislative branch had. So dominant had the chief executive's role become over the federal budget that when Nixon refused to spend money for housing and natural resource programs that Congress had appropriated, Congress was unable to make him spend the money. Although Nixon signed into law less than one month before he left office the Congressional Budget Act of 1974, many were wondering just who had the power of the purse in the early 1970s.

But as the anti-war protests grew and the

unraveling of the Nixon presidency through the Watergate scandals forced the resignation of the President in August of 1974, the congressional elections of that year resulted in the American people sending to Congress a group of officials determined to reassert the constitutional role of the legislative branch, especially in the realm of fiscal policy. The era of the imperial Presidency had ended. No longer would the legislative branch sign a blank check for the executive branch to spend.

Congress Reasserts Its Role
in the Governing Process

Known as the Watergate Baby Class, the new Democratic members elected to Congress in 1974 had an agenda for reform. Actually, older members such as Democratic member Richard Bolling of Missouri had been working for several years to change business in the House. Now he had the numbers in the new freshmen, most of whom had never held political office and many of whom had been anti-war

protesters and civil rights and environmental activists. They eagerly supported change in the House.

When the newly elected House members gathered in the late fall in Washington, the Democratic Caucus met and changed many of the rules. In an effort to break the power of the baronial committee chairmen, the seniority system for assuming the chairmanship of a committee was abolished. In addition to this, rules changes also brought about the creation of subcommittees for each full committee. This meant that most legislation had to be considered by the subcommittee first, another incursion to the almighty powers that had been wielded by the full committee chairmen for decades. Further rules changes brought the opening of congressional committee hearings to the public. Prior to this time, hearings, deals, and testimony had all occurred behind closed doors. It was hoped that having "government in the sunshine" would bring credibility back to the federal government in the wake of Watergate and the Vietnam War.

Because it lacked its own sources of information that could challenge, question, and critique the requests made by the executive for legislation and budget, Congress hired many more staff to work for the senators and representatives directly as well as for the committees and now for the subcommittees that had been created. Congress also decided to expand the size of the staff of the Library of Congress and the General Accounting Office, both support agency groups. It created the Office of Technology Assessment in order to have its own source of scientific information. Finally, the Budget Act of 1974 included the Congressional Budget Office (CBO), a support group that would advise Congress on the budget requests that the President submitted each year.

With the additional staff support, the CBO, and the new process set in place by the Budget Act of 1974, the legislative branch became more proactive in the matter of decisions over the federal budget that the President submitted each year to Capitol Hill. (See Chapter 4 for details about processes.)

From that time forward, Congress no longer would sign a blank check for the President to cash following his request each year in February. Lengthy discussion in Congress each year over the spending priorities and the taxes that are contained in the President's request has become part of the federal budget process in Washington.

From Jimmy Carter to Bill Clinton: Mid-1970s to 2000

The unchallenged position of the United States' economic dominance in the world came to an end in the "stagflation" decade of the 1970s. The bills from the Great Society programs of the 1960s and the Vietnam War came due. At the same time, the country experienced its first energy crisis when the Gulf States dramatically raised the price of a barrel of oil, which resulted in the doubling of the cost of a gallon of gasoline in the United States. Countries such as Japan and Germany, which had suffered industrial devastation during World War II, also were on their feet again with new technology and know-how. This forced the United States to face major economic competition for the first time since World War I.

The combination of the above factors, along with others, led to a period of high interest rates, terrible inflation, and growing unemployment. Jimmy Carter, president from 1977 to 1980, even though a Democrat, was unable to work with the Democratic Congress to alter this slide into economic demise. By the time the country was more than ready for the presidential elections of 1980, retired people were making more money from their benefits with COLAs indexed to the rate of inflation than were many people working full time.

The Ronald Reagan Revolution promised to cut government spending and waste, cut taxes, and build up defense to defeat the Soviet Union. Elected with him in 1980 was a Republican-controlled Senate - the

first one since 1952 - as well as a larger number of Republicans in the House. Although still controlled by the Democrats with Tip O'Neill as the speaker, the House now had enough conservative Democrats from the South and the Southwest who also believed quite strongly in the policies of the Reagan Revolution. Thus, the cuts in taxes and government spending that the Reagan White House proposed to Congress in 1981 passed both Houses of Congress. Many social programs were eliminated. The income taxes of middle class people were cut for three succeeding years as were the taxes of businesses and corporations. No one touched the entitlements, those programs that gave federal benefits automatically to anyone who qualified under the formula so outlined in the law.

One of the worst recessions in the country's history began in late 1981 and with it grew the deficits. When Jimmy Carter left office, the deficit for fiscal year 1980 was $60 billion. From 1981 - when the deficit broke $100 billion - until fiscal year 1996, the deficit remained over $100 billion and grew to its height of $290 billion in the early 1990s. Indeed, our country's deficits before 1981 paled in comparison to what followed. That year, the government cut income taxes and greatly increased defense spending, but did not cut non-defense programs enough to make up the difference. Also, the recession of the early 1980s reduced federal revenues, increased federal outlays for unemployment insurance and similar programs that are closely tied to economic conditions, and forced the government to pay interest on more national debt at a time when interest rates were high. As a result the deficit soared.

By 1990, President George H. W. Bush and Congress enacted spending cuts and tax increases that were designed to reduce the accumulated deficits by about $500 billion over five years. They also enacted the Budget Enforcement Act (BEA). Rather than set annual deficit targets, the BEA was designed to limit discretionary spending while ensuring that any new entitlement programs or tax cuts did not make the deficit worse.

For what it was designed to do, the law worked. It did, in fact, limit discretionary spending and force proponents of new entitlements and tax cuts to find ways to finance them. But the deficit, which government and private experts said would fall, actually rose.

Why? Because the recession of the early 1990s reduced individual and corporate tax revenues and increased spending that is tied to economic fluctuations (unemployment benefits, Food Stamps). Federal health care spending also continued to grow rapidly.

In 1993, President Clinton and the Congress made another effort to decrease the deficit. They enacted a five-year deficit reduction package of spending cuts and higher revenues. The law was designed to cut the accumulated deficits from 1994 to 1998 by about $500 billion. The new law extended the caps on discretionary spending as well as the entitlement controls enacted in the BEA.

It seems that President Clinton's deficit reduction efforts paid off. The deficit fell from $290 billion in 1992 to $107 billion in 1996 and was as low as $37 billion for 1997. The deficit also fell by two-thirds as a share of the Gross Domestic Product (GDP) to 1.4 percent. For the following four fiscal years, the federal government ran surpluses because of the tax increases in 1990 and 1993 in addition to the increased revenues from capital gains taxes because of the boom in the stock market.

In the summer of 1997, President Clinton and Congress agreed to a budget plan that would balance the budget by 2002. They also agreed to the largest tax cut for some American people since 1981. For the first time, the politicians at both ends of Pennsylvania Avenue were trying to reduce the costs of entitlements such as Medicare and Medicaid. Is the country really getting its fiscal house in order for the 21st century? There seemed to be a consensus in Washington those days to work together to do this.

The Federal Budget during the Presidency of George W. Bush

When George W. Bush campaigned for the White House, he promised to cut taxes. With federal budget surpluses predicted for as many as 10 years, he felt that a large tax cut was in order. In the spring of 2001, the Republican controlled House of Representatives, largely along party lines, passed President Bush's tax cut. A few months later, the Senate also passed the tax cut.

The first budget submitted by President George W. Bush contained large tax cuts, mainly for the wealthy, that were passed in June, 2001. After the tragedy of 9/11 that year, the budget for 2002 passed with little controversy. Congressional action on the President's budget request for 2003 broke down completely. Unable to pass appropriation bills by October 1, 2002, a series of continuing resolutions was passed to keep the government open while lawmakers made final decisions on the 2003 budget in the early months of 2003.

For FY 2004, Congress completed work on the budget in January of 2004, several months after the fiscal year began on October 1, 2003.

By the end of George W. Bush's first term, the nation's debt had increased to more than $8 trillion, more than $2 trillion since he became

president in 2001. His tax cuts, the war on terrorism and the wars in Afghanistan and Iraq all contributed to this debt, but so also had spending by Congress.

For FY 2009, 61 percent of the $3.1 trillion requested by the President was for mandatory spending with the remaining 39 percent for discretionary, appropriated spending or $1,212,000,000. Of this latter amount, $730,000,000 is for defense and homeland security with $482,000,000 left for natural resources and the environment, transportation, education, labor and health programs. The question in Washington was where can the cuts occur?

In the late summer and early fall of 2008, the growing home mortgage crisis spread throughout the entire economy leading to the worst national fiscal and economic crisis that the United States (and the world) has faced since the 1930s. Congress rejected the initial proposal to save the country's financial institutions sent to Capitol Hill by the head of the Federal Reserve, Benjamin Bernanke and Henry Paulson, President Bush's last Secretary of the Treasury. By early October, a $700 billion package passed Congress with the understanding that these federal dollars (tax payers' money) would aid those losing their homes as a result of the sub-prime mortgage debacle. In the end, Secretary Paulson spent $350 billion allotted by Congress to save large institutions such as A.I.G., the world's largest insurance company, and Bank of America, leaving $350 billion for the new president, who was to be elected in November.

Barack Obama Comes to Power

 On January 20, 2009, Barack Obama became the 44th President of the United States. The fiscal and economic problems that his administration faces are daunting. The realities of huge deficits and a growing national debt may inhibit President Obama's plans for health care for all Americans and energy independence from foreign sources of oil. As of the publication of this book, the $787 billion stimulus package has been passed by the 111th Congress with only three Republicans in the Senate voting for it. Trying to end the bitter rancor of partisanship in Washington, DC on Capitol Hill in the face of a possible devastating economic crisis presents a major challenge for the new Obama administration.

A year to the day of anniversary of his inauguration, January 20, 2010, unemployment in the country remained at 10%.

2 THE EXECUTIVE AND LEGISLATIVE BRANCHES AND HOW THE FEDERAL BUDGET IS MADE

The uniqueness of the separation of powers in the U.S. Government can be seen quite well in the federal budget making process in Washington. As noted previously, the Founding Fathers who wrote the Constitution did not trust human nature and thus designed a government in which power was balanced among three branches of government, each with the ability to check the power of the other. Nowhere is this capacity to check another branch seen as clearly as in the power of the purse held by Congress - the legislative branch. Every year, the President - the chief executive of the United States - must ask Congress for money to fund the operations of the U. S. Government. How well we know that conflict between these two branches can exist as many recall the shutdown of the federal government for nearly a month in the winter of 1995-1996. The difficulty of reaching a consensus about budget levels was again brought to the public's attention in 2011. Repeated threats to shut down the government due to insufficient funds were averted by final hour stopgap measures resulting from agreements between President Obama and the 112th U.S. Congress. A look at how the federal budget is made each year provides a good review of the federal government's operations.

Operationally, power on Capitol Hill can be found in many places. There are 535 voting members of Congress who have at least that number of ideas about the budget. Power flows in a rather horizontal way, from political party leaders from committee chairmen and chairwomen, from party caucuses, and even from constituents. With power in so many places, some have said that Congress is "organized" but is it "led?" The following Constitutional language outlines Congress's power of the purse:

Article I: Section 8
Clause 1. The Congress shall have Power to lay and collect Taxes, Duties, Imposts and Excises, to pay the Debts and provide for the common Defense and general Welfare of the United States...

Article I: Section 9
Clause 7. No Money shall be drawn from the Treasury, but in Consequence of Appropriations made by Law...

In contrast to the dispersed nature of congressional power, operationally, power and direction of government function for the executive branch flows from the White House, from the office of the President. Power flows vertically with the President being the source of the power. The following Constitutional authorities underpin the President's responsibilities that have budget implications:

Article II: Section 2

Clauses 1 and 2. The president shall be Commander in Chief...He shall have Power, by and with the Advice and Consent of the Senate, to make Treaties... and shall appoint Ambassadors, other public Ministers and Consuls, Judges of the supreme court...

Article II: Section 3

Clause 1. He shall from time to time give to the Congress Information of the State of the Union, and recommend to their Consideration such Measures as he shall judge necessary and expedient.

Budget of the U.S. Government
Its Purpose

Presidential candidates make promises on the campaign trail that they hope to fulfill if elected to the White House. A promise, such as affordable health care for all Americans made by candidate Barack Obama, may become part of a president's policy agenda, a promise that will cost money. Thus, a President's annual budget request to Congress contains his priorities for spending for the nation, guns for defense and/or butter for social programs.

The budget request submitted by the President also contains the dollars needed to run the federal bureaucracy. The federal bureaucracy is supported by more than one million civilian civil servants (those bureaucrats) and a professional military of nearly two million. The salaries and benefits of these public servants as well as the financial resources needed to support their programs (equipment and administrative overhead) must be requested in the President's budget for a fiscal year.

Its Scope

Up until the fall of 2008, the budget of the federal government represented about $3.1 trillion or about 20 percent of the country's gross domestic product (GDP) of $15 trillion. The 2008 fiscal and economic crises shrank the size of the GDP. To appreciate the size of the federal budget, the combined outlay budgets of all state governments in 2008 equaled $689.5 billion.

Since the federal budget provides services and benefits for a nation of more than 310 million people, its sheer size and scope affects the country's economy and the lives of most Americans. Whether providing for defense and homeland security, the social benefits of Social Security and Medicare, economic aid and stimulus policies, or crop subsidies for the American farmers, just about everyone is touched by the dollars that flow from Washington.

Budget Terminology

What should be noted at the outset of this discussion is that the budget process is an ongoing one, that there is no beginning and there is no end. The federal government's fiscal year (FY) begins on October 1 and ends on September 30 of the following calendar year.

Simultaneously throughout any fiscal year, four fiscal years' budgets are being worked on either by the executive or the legislative branch of the U.S. Government. Whenever discussion of the federal budget takes place, one should always ask the question: "Which fiscal year are we talking about?" (See Table on page 48.) For example, in the spring of each calendar year, while

What Congressional and Executive Agency Processes Are Going on in FY 2012

October - December
Start of New Fiscal Year

Fiscal Year 2012 Begins.

OMB Reviews agency requests for FY 2013 and issues passbacks; agency appeals to OMB and/or President. Final decisions.

Field offices developing budget estimates for FY 2014.

January - February

Congressional Review of agencies FY 2011 accomplishments.

Compililation and printing of executive budget request for FY 2013. President submits budget request to Congress no later than the first Monday in February.

March - June

Executives agencies implement programs for FY 2012.

Congressional consideration of the President's budget request begins. March 15 Committees submit views and estimates on the budget to budget committee. April 15 Deadline for adopting the budget resolution for FY 2013.

Development of budget guidelines and preliminary policies. Call for estimates issued by agency budget office to operating units.

July - September

Appropriations process (Congress writes budget). May - July House action on regular appropriations bills for FY 2013. July - September Senate action and conference on regular appropriations; enactment of appropriations.

Agencies formulate detailed request for FY 2014, which are submitted to OMB.

48

the executive branch is beginning the formulation of a budget for submission to Congress for the following February, federal agencies who work for the President are implementing the budget Congress has given them for the current fiscal year. At the same time that the executive is planning for one budget year and implementing the current fiscal year's budget, the legislative branch is writing the budget for the fiscal year that begins on October 1 and reviewing agencies' accomplishments achieved in the budget year that ended the previous September.

In other words, in the spring of 2012, the bureaucracy in the executive branch is implementing the budget given it for 2012 while formulating the budget request for fiscal year (FY) 2014. At the same time, Congress, through congressional hearings, is writing the budget for FY 2013 and reviewing the annual reports of accomplishments by the executive branch for FY 2011.

Where the Money Comes From

The money that the federal government uses to pay it's bills - it's revenues - comes mostly from taxes.

In recent years, revenues have been lower than spending, and the government has borrowed to finance the difference between revenues and spending (the deficit).

Revenue for FY 2013, is projected to be $3,003

trillion, $376 billion more than 2012.

Revenues come from the following sources:

FIGURE 2: FY 2013 Budget Request
Where the Money Comes From

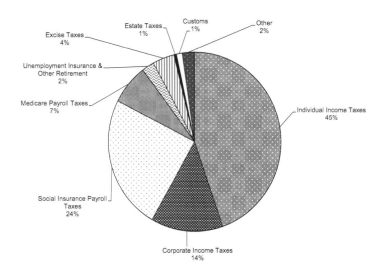

- Individual income taxes will raise an estimated $1,344 trillion in 2013. This is an increase of $203 billion from 2012.
- Social insurance payroll taxes include Social Security taxes, Medicare taxes, unemployment insurance taxes, and federal employee retirement payments. This category amounts to $1,016 trillion for 2013, $89 billion more than 2012.
- Corporate income taxes that will raise an estimated $405 billion in 2012 have risen as a percent of the GDP. The increase from 2012 to 2013 is $76 billion.

- Excise taxes apply to various products, including alcohol, tobacco, transportation fuels, and telephone services. The government earmarks some of these taxes to support certain activities, including highways, airports, and airways, and the cleanup of hazardous substances, and deposits others in the general fund. This accounts for 4 percent of the revenue budget, equating to $121 billion for FY 2013.
- The government also collects miscellaneous revenues such as customs duties (in the 1880s this was the our primary source of revenue), Federal Reserve earnings, fines, penalties, estate taxes, and forfeitures equaling 4 percent of the budget or $101 billion for FY 2013. This includes a new allowance for health reform.

Where the Money Goes

As of this printing for fiscal year 2013, President Barack Obama is projected to request approval of a budget of almost $3.8 trillion.

But there are still basically two categories of spending by the executive branch, namely mandatory and discretionary. Mandatory spending is for programs the level of which is governed by formulas or criteria set forth in authorizing legislation rather than appropriations. Medicare and veterans' pensions are examples of such programs. Discretionary spending covers those areas for spending on a yearly or multiyear basis that are at Congress' discretion and lie in the jurisdiction of the appropriations committees. The breakout for both mandatory and discretionary spending follows:

FIGURE 3: FY 2013 Budget Request
Where the Money Goes

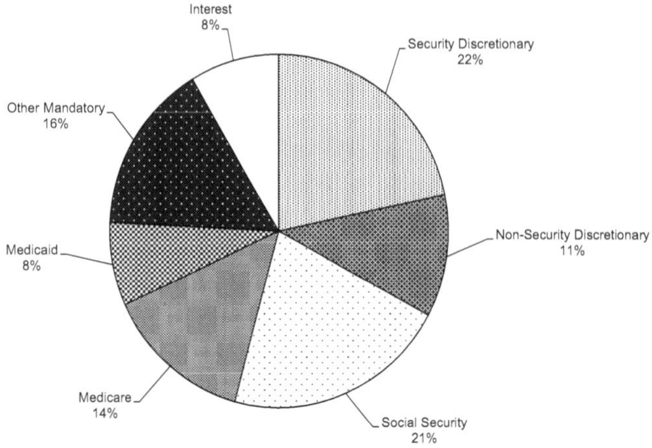

Mandatory

- The largest federal program is Social Security, which provides monthly benefits to more than 49 million retired and disabled workers, their dependents, and survivors. It accounts for 21 percent of all federal spending or $802 billion for FY 2013.
- Medicare, which provides health care coverage for over 42 million elderly Americans and people with disabilities, consists of Part A (hospital insurance) and Part B (insurance for

physician costs and other services). In 2003, the Republican controlled congress passed, and President George W. Bush signed, Medicare Part D that funds prescriptions for the elderly. Since its creation in 1965, Medicare has accounted for an ever-growing share of spending. In 2013 it will amount to 14 percent of the federal budget or $528 billion.

• Medicaid provides health care services to over 34 million Americans, including the poor with disabilities and senior citizens in nursing homes. Unlike Medicare, the federal government shares the costs of Medicaid with the states, paying between 50 and 83 percent of the total (depending on each state's requirements). Federal and state costs are growing rapidly. Medicaid accounts for 8 percent of the federal budget in FY 2013 or $288 billion.

• Other means-tested entitlements provide benefits to people and families with incomes below certain minimum levels that vary from program to program. The major means-tested entitlements are U.S. Food Stamps and food aid to Puerto Rico, Supplemental Security Income (SSI), child nutrition, the earned income tax credit, and veterans' pensions. The remaining entitlements mainly consist of federal retirement and insurance programs, and payments to farmers. Due to the financial housing and unemployment crises of 2008, along with the bailout of the financial institutions, this category increased in 2012. The proposed 2013 budget however does not budget for federal government bailing out financial institutions. Accordingly, the means tested entitlements for FY2013 is expected to decrease to 16 percent or $583 billion.

- Interest payments, primarily the result of previous budget deficits, averaged 7 percent of federal spending in the 1960s and 1970s. Due to the large budget deficits that began in the 1980s, that share quickly doubled to 14 percent. Interest payments on the debt were declining in the years of budget surplus from 1998-2001. However, with the recession of 2001, the tax cuts in 2001 and 2003, wars in Iraq and Afghanistan, the hurricane catastrophes of 2004 and 2005 and the financial crisis of 2008 interest payments on the debt for 2013 are projected to be $321 billion or 8.5 percent. This is a 2 percent increase over 2012 ($79 billion).

Add up these percentages and you will find that the mandatory side of the spending totals 67 percent of the entire budget! Checks are written automatically each month to pay these benefits and to pay the interest on the debt.

Discretionary

- National Security discretionary spending will total an estimated $819 billion in 2013, comprising 22 percent of the budget, declining 2 percent from 2012. Homeland Security is now included in the National Security line item.
- Non-defense discretionary spending is a wide array of programs that include education, training, science, technology, housing, transportation, and foreign aid and some grants to states and localities for FY 2013 will total $423 billion or 11 percent of the total budget request, $33 billion less than FY 2012 and a drop of 1.5%.

Discretionary, appropriated dollars - both defense and non-defense - represent only 33 percent of the entire budget. This part of the budget is subject to yearly scrutiny through the appropriations process in Congress. The discretionary part of the federal budget pie is quite likely where your interests in federal spending lie. At only 33 percent, it also represents about $1,243 trillion that the government will spend in the next fiscal year.

Action of Capitol Hill

It should be noted here that the "budget" Congress acts on in a given year is not a single document. Total

Table 5.

CBO's Baseline Budget Projections

In Billions of Dollars

	Actual 2008	2009	2010	2011	2012	2013	2014	2015	2016	2017	2018	2019	Total, 2010-2014	Total, 2010-2019
Revenues														
Individual income taxes	1,146	1,060	1,199	1,396	1,572	1,726	1,853	1,978	2,099	2,227	2,347	2,473	7,745	18,870
Corporate income taxes	304	223	252	290	333	343	334	347	347	349	353	355	1,553	3,304
Social insurance taxes	900	915	938	978	1,032	1,087	1,141	1,192	1,242	1,294	1,347	1,403	5,176	11,653
Other	173	160	144	162	187	197	216	229	241	253	262	272	906	2,164
Total Revenues	2,524	2,357	2,533	2,825	3,124	3,353	3,544	3,746	3,929	4,122	4,309	4,505	15,380	35,991
On-budget	1,866	1,686	1,846	2,111	2,372	2,561	2,710	2,873	3,019	3,173	3,320	3,476	11,600	27,461
Off-budget	658	672	687	714	752	793	834	873	910	949	989	1,029	3,780	8,530
Outlays														
Mandatory spending	1,597	2,164	1,857	1,914	1,906	2,033	2,156	2,298	2,458	2,572	2,694	2,900	9,865	22,758
Discretionary spending	1,133	1,184	1,188	1,189	1,193	1,220	1,246	1,274	1,308	1,335	1,362	1,399	6,036	12,714
Net interest	299	195	191	220	289	358	392	418	434	448	452	451	1,450	3,654
Total Outlays	2,978	3,543	3,236	3,323	3,388	3,610	3,794	3,980	4,201	4,355	4,497	4,740	17,351	39,126
On-budget	2,504	3,026	2,689	2,752	2,784	2,973	3,121	3,271	3,453	3,565	3,663	3,857	14,320	32,129
Off-budget	475	517	547	571	604	637	672	709	748	790	835	883	3,031	6,997

federal revenues and spending each year stem from many provisions in existing law enacted by previous Congresses (i.e., the tax cuts of 2001 and 2003, Medicare payments).

Congress also has its own budget office, the Congressional Budget Office (CBO), that also provides information and input on an annual requested budget as well as projections for budget in the out years. On the previous page is an example of CBO information. (Source: Congressional Budget Office, The Budget and Economic Outlook: Fiscal Years 2009 to 2019, January 2008, Table 5, p. 56.).

3 | THE FEDERAL BUDGET AND THE EXECUTIVE BRANCH

The budget formulation process by the executive branch involves the simultaneous consideration of the resource needs of individual programs, the allocation of resources among the functions of the government, the total outlays and receipts that are appropriate in relation to current and prospective economic conditions, and statutory constraints. The formulation of the President's budget begins about 18 months before the fiscal year under consideration. This means that in March 2010, the executive branch began planning for the 2012 budget, which should begin on October 1, 2011.

Each year in the late winter and early spring, bureaucrats in the executive branch's agencies and departments submit their requests to their program and budget offices for activities they wish to be funded. After many months of negotiations among the White House, Office and Management (OMB), and the agencies, the President's budget request is submitted to Capitol Hill in early February of each year.

If the United States had a parliamentary form of government, approval of the budget by the legislative branch would be immediate. The chief executive in parliamentary government holds his or her position because he is the leader of the party that has the majority of seats in the lawmaking body of the government. He or she (remember Margaret Thatcher) is also a member of the legislative body. Under this system, however, there is no separation of powers between the executive and legislative branches like that which exists in the United States.

The Constitution calls for the legislative branch to be the revenue-raising arm of the government (see pages 36-37). Over the years, Congress also has become very involved in the appropriating process. Thus, a federal budget request that is submitted to Capitol Hill with the politics and legislative agenda of one individual behind it, the President, encounters the legislative agendas and parochial interests of the 535 members of Congress. Let's take a closer look at this formulation of the President's budget request each year and where you may have some input.

The Executive Branch and the Players

The Department of the Treasury

If you look at the "White House campus," the building for the Department of the Treasury is right next door to the White House. Critical to participation in the executive branch budget process, the Treasury Department oversees the Internal Revenue Service, the bureau that collects the federal tax revenues for the United States of America. Without tax as well as congressional appropriated dollars, the federal government cannot function. Note: Of course, Congress is the source of the tax  law that generates revenues for the federal government. Thus there are taxes in every budget request that is sent by the President to Capitol Hill for annual consideration and appropriation. For example, the budget request contains the permanent payroll taxes that pay for the Social Security and Medicare benefits for the elderly. There are estimates for the revenues from the federal gasoline tax as well as other revenue or tax sources (see Figure 2, page 50).

The Treasury Department also oversees the bonded debt of the United States. It conducts sales of U.S. Treasury bonds on a quarterly basis to help fund the debt of the United States. In the fall of 2008, Congress passed and George W. Bush signed a bailout bill of $700 billion for a bailout of the financial institutions of the country to be administered by the Department of the Treasury.

Office of Management and Budget

A major player in the Executive Office of the President is the Office of Management and Budget, known as OMB, which is located in a building next to the White House. Serving as a critical support in his budget and managing efforts of the huge bureaucracy, the President's budget office oversees the budget request formulation each year before it is sent to Capitol Hill. The process starts with budget guidance issued by OMB to all agencies and ends with the President's budget request to Congress. The director of OMB, a political appointee and also of cabinet level status, makes sure that the details of the budget request reflect the policies of the President.

Currently, the five general divisions within OMB that oversee the budgets of various departments and agencies include General Government and Finance, Health and Personnel, Human Resources, National Security and International Affairs, and Natural Resources, Energy, and Science. Funding issues for NASA and the National Park Service would come under the last division, with foreign aid and defense funding under National Security and International Affairs.

Assisting in the number crunching to make the budget request are the career civil servants known as budget examiners who work in the various divisions and branches at OMB. Bright and dedicated, they work with the civil servants within the bureaucracy to put together the Presidents's budget request.

The forerunner of OMB was the Bureau of the Budget, which was created by Congress in 1921 with the passage of the Budget and Accounting Act. Following World War I, Congress thought that the bureaucracy had performed so well for the war effort that the President should know how much money was needed to fund the executive branch each year. Prior to 1921, a single "Book of Estimates" composed of individual departments' submissions was sent by the executive branch to Capitol Hill. Every agency head and cabinet secretary lobbied Congress individually to ask for money.

Today, about 200 budget examiners work in various branches in OMB to examine carefully each agency's request for money for the fiscal year that will begin on October 1. Their job is to look for cuts in requests. A critical role that OMB plays in budget formulation is linking the dollars requested by departments and agencies to the President's stated policy agenda. At the same time they are also looking to see what Congress has cut, increased, or left alone in the President's budget request that was submitted to Capitol Hill in the previous February for the upcoming fiscal year.

For years the executive branch submitted the annual budget request to Congress in January. The deadline changed in 1990. Since then, from the fall to early February, when the President submits his budget to Congress, information for the upcoming budget request is privileged, not at all public. Those agencies that do not agree with the cuts that the OMB examiners may have made in their budgets may go through a "reclama" or appeals process to have the requested funds reinstated. The President's budget is normally submitted to Congress on the first Monday in February when congressional action begins to write a budget for the next fiscal year.

Executive Branch Agencies.

Even though Congress has the power of the purse, discussion for an upcoming fiscal year's budget begins at the White House. Remember that most presidents have been elected to the White House having made promises that more often than not mean programs that will cost money. While Ronald Reagan promised to cut the budget, he asked for and received more than $1 trillion from Congress to fund programs for the Department of Defense.

Currently there are 15 cabinet level secretaries in addition to the Attorney General who run huge areas of the federal government. The departments that these politically appointed people run are as follows:

- Agriculture
- Commerce
- Defense
- Education
- Energy
- Health & Human Services
- Homeland Security
- Housing & Urban Development
- Interior
- Justice
- Labor
- State
- Transportation
- Treasury
- Veterans Affairs

Each one of these departments also has many agencies with program offices within them. For example, in the Department of Defense, there is the Navy that has agencies such as NAVSEA and NAVAIR where ships and airplanes are overseen, respectively. Within the Department of the Interior, there is the U.S. Fish and Wildlife Service, the National Park Service, the Bureau of Reclamation, and the U.S. Geological Survey. The responsibilities of the Justice Department range from the Bureau of Alcohol, Tobacco and Firearms to the Federal Bureau of Prisons. All of these agencies within these cabinet-level departments must submit a budget request for each fiscal year. There are literally thousands of them within the federal government and not all of them are located in Washington. Some may be in your city or town.

Many of the federal government's functions within these agencies and departments work with discretionary funding, that part of the budget that is allocated on a yearly basis (see figure 3, page 42). Citizen input may be had here for increased funding with the local park ranger, for example, when the budget formulation season takes place. Remember, even though the secretaries of HUD or Commerce are political appointees whose job it is to support the Presidents's policies in the areas of their jurisdiction, the thousands of civil servants who work to put a budget together on a yearly basis are there for their careers, know the budget well, and are on your payroll. They work for you.

Executive branch agencies have the numbers from the previous and current year's budget from which many budget planners begin their work. By the beginning of the summer, OMB has released general budget guidelines throughout the executive branch. The guidance factors include technical economic assumptions (unemployment, inflation, the size of the deficit). Anywhere from 18 months to two years may pass from the time the agencies begin the work on a fiscal year's budget until final passage by Congress. In Washington, the spring is a very busy time for budget formulation among agencies.

But also realize that many federal field offices, whether national forests or naval aviation depots, have submitted numbers to Washington by February and that their process may have begun as early as the previous fall. In the spring of each year, some 18 months before the start of a new fiscal year, federal departments and agencies assess their budget needs and priorities. It is at this time that initial citizen input can be made. Budget direction for some agencies takes place solely at the Washington office with little input from the field offices.

But often there are instances where budget formulation begins with input from the field offices. For example, operating with the current fiscal year dollars, the superintendent of a national park, the manager of a wildlife refuge, and the director of the new probe for Mars at a NASA lab evaluate their workloads and the resources needed to achieve their goals as outlined in the agency's strategic plan. Staying even with inflation, but also, perhaps, desirous to expand services in some capacity, they put together their budget requests. If field units are involved, often their numbers and requests must arrive in Washington by February before the spring assessments by other agencies.

By late July or early August, agency heads make their case to a department's secretary. Much like committee hearings on Capitol Hill, the director of the National Park Service and the Secretary of the Navy, for example, must justify their figures for the fiscal year's budget that is being formulated before the secretary of Interior or Defense respectively. Remember, the Secretary of Interior or Defense may present to OMB only one budget request for his or her department. Thus, competition for dollars is often great among the various agencies within a department. A Secretary may also have received White House (OMB) direction for spending priorities for the fiscal year.

Once an entire department's budget is finalized, its secretary must then make a budget presentation to the Office of Management and Budget (OMB), the

President's budget office. This usually occurs in September right after Labor Day.

After Labor Day and into the early fall, the budget examiners or resource management officers at OMB, who have received the requests from the departments and agencies assess the requests. They will analyze these requests and write a report for the director's review. Potential controversial items will be presented to the director for resolution by the examiners. These examiners can have a great deal of line-item clout over an agency's budget. Always conscious of the President's policy agenda, OMB structures the budget request to reflect this agenda.

At this stage of the process, and actually since the formulation of budget requests, the budget is the privileged information of the executive branch. It is not open to public input or comment until it is submitted to Congress in early February, eight months before the start of the fiscal year under consideration.

GPRA

With the passage of the Government Performance and Results Act (GPRA) in 1993, federal agencies will be forming budgets based on their five-year strategic plans. The act requires that agencies identify their mission and how they plan to achieve it by measuring their performance through the strategic plan. More mission based than needs based, desired projects by citizens', industry, or international groups could be a part of an agency's plan.

Executive Budget Goes to Capitol Hill

Congress reconvenes in January of each year. The President submits his budget request for congressional consideration in early February. With over a year of preparation by the executive branch, the legislative branch now has eight months to examine and write a budget for the upcoming fiscal year that begins on October 1st.

Any new program that a department, agency, or lobbying or international group may want funded should be in the President's budget request when it is sent to Capitol Hill. Executive agencies along with interest groups have many months to try to incorporate funds for their projects into the budget before the President submits his request to Congress. Funding for new projects after the budget has reached the Hill is very difficult to incorporate.

Transition of a President

One important exception is that the current timing does not require an outgoing President to transmit a budget, and it is impractical for an incoming President to complete a budget request within a few days of taking office on January 20th. President Clinton, the first President subject to the current requirement, submitted a report to

Congress on February 17, 1993, which described a comprehensive economic plan he proposed for the nation and which also contained summary budget information. He transmitted the "Budget of the United States for 1994" on April 8, 1993.

In other years, Presidents have submitted abbreviated budget documents on the due date, sending the more detailed documents weeks later. For the 1997 budget, President Clinton transmitted a document to Congress on February 5, 1996, that provided a thematic overview of his priorities and the administration's latest economic assumptions. Because of the uncertainty over the 1996 appropriations due to government shutdowns as a result of the disagreements between the Democrat-controlled White House and the Republican-controlled Congress, as well as possible changes in mandatory programs and tax policy, OMB was unable to provide by that date all of the material normally contained in the President's budget. That material was transmitted in mid-March of 1996.

When George W. Bush became president, his initial budget request was later than usual because of the delay in determining the 2000 presidential election results. The full budget request arrived on Capitol Hill late in the spring in 2001.

President Barack Obama's administration followed that of those in previous years with a "skeleton" budget submitted in early February with a more complete version to be submitted in the spring that will contain President Obama's legislative priorities for discretionary spending. It should be pointed out that with over two-thirds of the budget already committed to mandatory spending, such a submission in early February should not be difficult.

Strategies for Input Into the Executive Budget Request

Now that we have outlined for you the budget formulation process, the players, and the time line within the executive branch, what follows are some practical tips to help you, the citizen, access the process.

1. Go to the field office of a federal agency and talk with the local federal officials about their programs that interest you.
2. Talk to the budget officer to learn the funding levels for the current fiscal year to make a plan for future dollars.
3. Show the officials that your idea or program plan will help meet the needs for the agency's overall strategic plan.
4. Provide support for the idea that will be convincing to top agency management and the budget office.
5. Provide information in a way that may convince OMB as well.

4 | THE CONGRESSIONAL BUDGET PROCESS

Now that you have an understanding of the formulation of a fiscal year's budget request by the executive branch, we will next look at congressional examination of this request. Remember before we begin, the executive branch spends anywhere from 10 to 18 months preparing a budget request for a fiscal year. Literally thousands of civil servants have input. A district ranger on a national forest in northern Idaho, a comptroller at an Army base in Germany, and the deputy chief of mission at the American consulate in Senegal all are involved in the process as they make the requests for their budgets to their superiors. When the proposed budget arrives on Congress' doorstep in early February of each year, the lawmakers and their staffs have eight months to examine it and to develop and pass a budget for the upcoming fiscal year.

In 1974 Congress passed the Congressional Budget and Impoundment Control Act in an effort to have greater influence over the course and content of the national budget. Reacting to the power of the "imperial presidencies" of Lyndon B. Johnson and

Richard Nixon as well as negative public opinion toward Washington in the wake of the Vietnam conflict and Watergate, the lawmakers on Capitol Hill felt that the legislative branch needed to reassert its constitutional right to control the country's purse strings. Responding to presidential initiatives, especially in budget matters, and not proposing its own throughout the 1960s, had eroded the power of Congress over the budget. In the years prior to 1974, power was only in a few places on Capitol Hill, thus enabling the White House to deal with only a few members, particularly senior members of Congress, to pass its programs.

During the years when the economics of deficit spending was the national way of doing government business, both for Republican and Democratic presidents, there were no committees on Capitol Hill monitoring the bottom line of expenditures versus revenues. Programs were created by the authorizing committees, funded by the appropriations committees, and implemented by the executive branch with little regard for tax revenues to pay for the government's services.

Along with this near automatic budget approval process on Capitol Hill, both the Johnson and Nixon administrations oversaw the creation of new entitlement programs, which meant greater government spending for people's needs. Johnson's Great Society initiatives such as Medicare and Medicaid, and President Nixon's block grant programs of General Revenue Sharing, the Comprehensive Employment and Training Act, and Community Development exemplify the chief executive's legislative successes on Capitol Hill in those years, victories that meant greater government spending. It was not until the passage of the Budget Act in 1974 that Congress established "tally sheets" to consider the budget.

The lack of institutional means to oversee the budget combined with the impoundment of funds by Nixon led concerned lawmakers to conceive and pass the Budget Act of 1974. The act made these changes:

- The fiscal year (FY) would begin on October 1 rather than July 1 to give Congress more time to study and discuss the budget.
- House and Senate budget committees would be established to set economic priorities by making spending recommendations to the appropriations and revenue-raising (tax) committees, thereby imposing a discipline on the budgeting process.
- The Congressional Budget Office (CBO) would be created to provide Congress with data and objective in-house advice for spending and taxes. (CBO serves Congress in much the same manner as the Office of Management and Budget [OMB] serves the President.)
- Congress would have the right to review and approve proposed presidential impoundment of funds.

- Congress would follow a timetable for budget passage.
-

TABLE 1: Congressional Budget Process Timetable

Time Frame	Action
Five days before the President's budget submission	Congressional Budget Office (CBO) submits sequestration preview report
Within six weeks after President's budget submission	Committees submit views and estimates to House Budget Committee
April 15	Congress completes action on fiscal year budget resolution
May 15	A year's annual appropriations may be considered in the House in absence of a budget resolution
June 10	House Appropriations Committee reports last annual appropriations bill
June 30	House completes action on annual appropriations bills
Prior to July 1	The President must order a sequester within 15 days of enactment of appropriations that exceed a fiscal year's caps; if appropriations are enacted after July 1 that exceed that year's caps, the caps for the next fiscal year are lowered
July 15	President submits mid-session budget review to Congress
October 1	Fiscal year begins
Varies by year	Target adjournment date

Nearly 35 years have passed since Congress began working within the guidelines of the budget process. What this process is, how it has changed, and how it works will be outlined on the following pages. Understanding the basic process and how it works today will provide you with some vital tools to make your elected representatives in Congress more accountable to you for your tax dollars.

Congressional Budget Process

The guidelines established by the 1974 Budget Act called for a series of steps that, at the time, included procedures that would set total budget targets for spending for the next fiscal year. The process laid out a series of date-specific deadlines, starting in March and ending in September, for the lawmakers to meet its budget considerations over a six-month period.

For the first few fiscal years following 1974, Congress kept to its timetable. The members in both houses of Congress took the schedule quite seriously. Even Sen. John Stennis (D), who in the mid-1970s was chairperson of both the Senate Armed Services Committee and the Defense Subcommittee on Appropriations, abided by the dates and spending ceilings set by the Senate Budget Committee.

The process did not work well or smoothly in the face of growing deficits in the 1980s. Congress, which established this timetable, could ignore it, and this was exactly what happened. With no budget in place by October 1, the government was funded by continuing resolution. This last-minute scramble led to government shutdowns in the 1980s, and greatly frustrated executive branch planners whose projects could not be implemented because Congress had not voted the money for the programs.

In an effort to gain better control over the mounting deficit, Congress passed the Balanced Budget and Emergency Deficit Control Act, which President Ronald Reagan signed on December 12, 1985. The act called for the budget deficit, then $171.9 billion, to be reduced annually beginning with FY 1986, the goal being to eliminate the deficit by FY 1991. Reflecting the general sentiment that Congress lacks the political will to curb deficits through the processes created by the 1974 Budget and Impoundment Control Act, the new legislation included mandatory cuts to balance the budget by October 1990.

The Gramm-Rudman-Hollings bill, which was named for the three senators who sponsored it, monopolized much of the legislative agenda in the fall of 1985. It was originally offered as an amendment to a bill to raise the nation's debt ceiling to $2,079 trillion from $1,824 trillion. Failure to pass the bill by December 12, 1985, would have caused the United States to default for the first time in its history.

The highlights of the Gramm-Rudman-Hollings Act included: the goal of $0 in deficits for FY 1991; automatic cuts for nonexempt programs to be divided equally between defense and nondefense programs if Congress failed to meet deficit targets in a fiscal year; exemptions from automatic cuts (e.g., Social Security, Medicare, programs for the very poor such as Aid to Families with Dependent Children and food stamps, as well as interest on the national debt); and, suspension of automatic cuts in time of war.

On February 7, 1986, a special federal judicial panel in Washington, D.C., declared unconstitutional the automatic budget-cutting provision, called sequestration, of the Gramm-Rudman-Hollings budget-balancing law. It violated the Constitution's separation of powers by giving the decision-making power of the executive branch to a legislative branch official, the comptroller general, who is the director of the General Accounting Office (GAO). Since the comptroller general can be removed by Congress, this officer cannot have executive branch decision-making authority. On July 7, 1986, the Supreme

Court also ruled that the provision for automatic cuts was unconstitutional.

In the fall of 1987, Congress reinstated the sequestration process (Gramm-Rudman II), but stipulated that automatic cuts should be issued by the President with the recommendation of OMB. Congress also extended the $0 deficit budget goal to FY 1993.

During George H. W. Bush's presidency, deficits failed to decline. Conflicts between Capitol Hill and the White House in finding agreement on a budget solution mounted. In an effort to work for more meaningful control over national spending, congressional and presidential budget negotiators finally developed a new process as part of the budget for FY 1991. The 1990 budget agreement called for Congress to pass the Budget Enforcement Act of 1990, which altered the budget process once again.

During fiscal years 1991-1993, the government's discretionary spending (yearly appropriated dollars) was divided among defense, domestic, and international aid programs. Each category was subject to sequestration (automatic cuts) if the money appropriated over the next three fiscal years exceeded targets set by the budget agreement reached in the fall of 1990. If a congressional committee wanted to increase spending for any program in these three discretionary areas, cuts had to come from other programs in the category, or revenues had to be raised to fund the new spending through taxes or user fees.

In fiscal years 1994 and 1995, the three discretionary spending areas once again faced automatic cuts if the targets for yearly spending were exceeded. This was the original design of Gramm-Rudman-Hollings in 1985. Exempt from the automatic budget chopping block were the entitlement programs, such as Social Security and Medicare, the fastest growing budget items. Operation Desert Storm was funded from an account separate from that of defense.

Projection of the programmatic cost estimates as well as the new revenue estimates rests with OMB, the President's budget office. This task belonged to CBO and the Joint Committee on Taxation - information agents of Congress - before the 1990 budget agreement.

When Bill Clinton was elected president, he promised to halve the budget deficit in his first term. The Omnibus Budget Reconciliation Act of 1993 narrowly passed the 103rd Congress. Containing both spending cuts and tax increases, this plan for deficit reduction continued to freeze the caps for discretionary, appropriated spending for five years, or until 1998. The plan did not call for freezes on any of the entitlement programs. The budget deficit declined from a record $290 billion in 1992, the last year of George H. W. Bush's presidency, to less than $100 billion in FY 1996.

As a result of the congressional elections of 1994, the Republican Party gained control of both the House and Senate for the first time in 40 years. Feeling that the American people wanted less government, the Republicans in the House, guided by their election manifesto, "the Contract with America," that promised a balanced budget by the year 2002 - were determined to cut federal taxes and programs. Republicans in the Senate wanted to cut spending before taxes. These disagreements among the Republicans on Capitol Hill in the face of the Democrat-controlled White House led to two government shutdowns, one in the fall of 1995 and a longer, nearly four-week shutdown in the early winter of 1995-1996. The final action resulted in more cuts in appropriated, discretionary dollars of nearly $30 billion. No one dealt with the mandatory, uncontrollable entitlements.

Republicans took most of the blame for the impasse over the budget discussions in 1996, and the 1996 elections resulted in losses of seats in the House and a gain of only one seat in the Senate. The 1996 election also saw the re-election of Bill Clinton, once again revealing that the American people liked divided government in Washington.

During the 105th Congress, both Republicans and Democrats signed on to the goal of balancing the budget by 2002. The budget resolution for FY 1998 outlined the direction lawmakers hoped to take over five years to reach a $0 deficit. Actually, in less than a year, for FY 1998, the first of several years of surpluses appeared.

These surpluses disappeared after 2001 when Congress cut taxes four years in a row. In addition to this, deficits returned due to the recession, the wars in Iraq and Afghanistan, and the growth in Federal Health Care Programs.

The Four Phases of the Budget Process

With the passage of the Omnibus Budget Reconciliation Act of 1993, the 1974 budget process was amended and its timetable was changed. In order to impose control over Congress's annual budget consideration, it was hoped that the budget process would provide a means to control the actions of the authorization, appropriations, and tax committees.

It is important to establish from the start the different kinds of committees on Capitol Hill and their roles in the budget process. The authorization committees in the House and Senate passed the substantive legislation that provides for the mandatory spending programs for Medicare, Medicaid, Food Stamps, and Unemployment Benefits. The House and Senate appropriations_committees oversee the annual spending for the discretionary part of the budget. The House Ways and Means Committee and the Senate Finance Committee have jurisdiction over tax or revenue raising legislation. These last committees are also the source of the legislation that raises the debt or borrowing ceiling of the federal government.

I. *Executive Budget Goes to Capitol Hill*

Congressional consideration of the President's budget request begins in early February of each year. With over a year of preparation by the executive branch, the legislative branch now has eight months to examine and pass the budget. All House and Senate standing committees must submit "views and estimates" of expenditures for the coming year to the budget committees within six weeks after the President's submission, the first major deadline in the budget process and also the end of phase one. Hearings take place to which cabinet secretaries are invited to defend the President's budget request in a global, philosophical sense, to support increases or cuts in various programs. As a result of these hearings, the committees send reports to the Budget Committees in the House and Senate with their reactions to the testimony given by the President's leading political representatives.

Any new program that a department, agency, lobbying or international group may want funded should be in the President's budget when it is sent to Capitol Hill. Executive agencies, along with interest groups, have 10 months to try to incorporate funds for their projects into the budget before the President submits his request to Congress. Funding for new projects after the budget has reached the Hill is very difficult to incorporate.

Until the 104th Congress and the return of Republican control of the legislative branch for the first time in 40 years, most programs contained in the executive budget and in the committees' March reports to the budget committees stayed in the proposed budget document. However, with the drive to cut the federal government and to balance the budget by 2002, greater scrutiny took place over the request. But it is still true that Congress does not have the staff, the time, or the expertise to examine absolutely every part of the President's budget request.

II. *The Budget Resolution*

The budget resolution has played a part in the budget process since its inception. Its purpose is to facilitate major change in budget policy, to allocate budget resources to congressional committees, and to begin the reconciliation process if necessary. The resolution will contain spending estimates for the next five fiscal years.

Between late February and April 15th, the deadline for passing the budget resolution, the House and Senate budget committees draft their versions of the budget resolution. Desirous of a budget that meets agreed-to targets in both discretionary and entitlement areas, these committees review the standing committees' proposed expenditures, the estimated tax revenues, and the CBO budget analysis to ensure that planned spending conforms to targets set in the budget agreements of prior years. Both houses should pass budget resolutions by April 15th, with differences between the two resolved in conference committee. If a budget resolution is not reported by this date, the budget committees set spending limits for appropriations committees in discretionary categories that equal those set in the President's original budget submission. These spending limits on appropriations are referred to as deeming resolutions when there is a difference in number of the Senate and House versions of the budget resolution and no agreement has been made.

In the spring of 1997, determined to come to a bipartisan agreement, the leaders in both the White House and the Congress agreed in principal to the budget plan for FY 1998 which outlined the moves toward a balanced budget by 2002. Right before the August recess on July 31st, three and one half months after the April 15th deadline, Congress overwhelmingly agreed to this plan. But remember, the President cannot sign this legislative vehicle, a resolution. It was simply an internal congressional working document to guide them in their final deliberations for the budget for FY 1998.

During the second session of the 107th Congress, Congress failed to pass a budget resolution. In that election year of 2002, the Democrats controlled the

Senate and the Republicans controlled the House. With no general plan for spending, the appropriations process broke down which resulted in numerous continuing resolutions until the 2003 budget was agreed to in the winter of 2003, over four months into the new fiscal year.

In 2007, the Democrats regained control of Congress. Disagreement with President Bush's overspending resulted in omnibus appropriations bills.

III. The Reconciliation Process

The annual budget resolution may contain directions, called reconciliation instructions, whose purpose it is to bring revenue and spending bills under existing laws within the jurisdiction of certain committees in line with the targets set in the budget resolution. Reconciliation is the process used by Congress to bring existing revenue and spending law into conformity with the policies of the budget resolution. It is used to change the amount of revenues, budget authority, or outlays generated by existing law. On the spending side, the process focuses on entitlement laws; it may not be used, however, to force changes in Social Security law.

The reconciliation bill contains instructions for certain committees in Congress to make changes in existing law.

Those committees that receive these instructions

have jurisdiction over entitlements (with the exception of Social Security), revenues (taxes), or user fees. The House Ways and Means and Senate Finance Committees are always involved in this process. Because of the caps in discretionary spending, outlined in each year's budget agreement, appropriations committees are usually not involved. For FY 1998, this process was used to cut the growth in spending for two entitlement programs over the next five years. The bill called for cuts in Medicare, the health care program for the elderly, of $115 billion and cuts in Medicaid, the health care program for the poor, of $13 billion.

Because under Senate rules a reconciliation bill can not be filibustered, only 51 votes are needed to pass a bill. As the 109th Congress began in January 2005, there was discussion that opening up the Arctic National Wildlife Refuge in Alaska for oil drilling (quite controversial in nature) would be placed in the reconciliation bill for FY 2006. Initially this measure passed with drilling for oil in Alaska. However, the final reconciliation bill for 2006 contained cuts in student loans, Medicaid, Farm and Energy Programs and nothing about opening up the Alaska Refuge.

IV. Authorization and Appropriations Processes

With an eye on the budget discussion for a given year, most of the work of the House and Senate authorization and appropriations committees takes place between mid-April and mid-September. Authorization committees are those committees that create federal programs that give the government its statutory authority to do its business. They do not have control over the amount of federal dollars released each year for spending. The authorization committees may also be involved in structuring the budget resolution, having submitted their views and estimates to the budget committees earlier in the year.

Those committees that control the discretionary, appropriated dollars are the appropriations committees, the committees that vote for the yearly spending for defense, NASA, and housing programs, for example. Because of the targets set by the Omnibus Budget Reconciliation Act of 1993 for discretionary categories, the appropriations committees already knew the ceilings in the respective categories for the next five years. Competition for discretionary dollars within the areas of domestic, defense, and international aid were greater than ever.

With the federal budget in surplus in the late 1990s and the tax on discretionary spending over, the Republican controlled Congress and the Democratic White House increased discretionary spending by billions of dollars. Prior to September 11, 2001, and the terrorist attacks on the United States, spending for national defense was projected by the CBO to grow more slowly than the non-defense part of the budget. Because of the war on terrorism, however, Congress voted $365 billion for defense in FY 2003 and President Bush's FY 2004 Budget requested $390 billion for defense. Such increase in defense meant fewer dollars for non-defense programs in future years. Thus competition and conflict for discretionary dollars was greater than ever.

Conflict between the authorizing and appropriating committees may also arise. To be funded, a program must be authorized, but this action does not guarantee funding. The appropriations committees may refuse or be unable to fund a program authorized by Congress in order to preserve targets set in a discretionary area for the upcoming fiscal year.

During the spring, agency officials appear before the House and Senate appropriations subcommittees to defend their budget requests and to offer plans for the department's future goals. Usually the full Committee on Appropriations accepts the recommendations of its subcommittees. As of February 2009, there were 12 subcommittees on appropriations in the House and 12 subcommittees on appropriations in the Senate.

They are as follows:

House Committee on Appropriations Subcommittees

1. Agriculture, Rural Development, Food and Drug Administration and Related Agencies
2. Commerce, Justice, Science and Related Agencies
3. Defense
4. Energy and Water Development
5. Financial Services and General Government
6. Homeland Security
7. Interior, Environment, and Related Agencies
8. Labor, Health and Human Services, Education, and Related Agencies
9. Legislative Branch
10. Military Construction, Veterans' Affairs, and Related Agencies
11. State, Foreign Operations and Related Programs
12. Transportation, Housing and Urban Development and Related Agencies

Senate Committee on Appropriations Subcommittees

1. Agriculture, Rural Development, Food and Drug Administration, and Related Agencies
2. Commerce, Justice, Science and Related Agencies
3. Defense
4. Energy and Water Development
5. Financial Services and General Government
6. Homeland Security
7. Interior, Environment, and Related Agencies
8. Labor, Health and Human Services, Education, and Related Agencies
9. Legislative Branch
10. Military Construction, Veterans' Affairs and Related Agencies
11. State, Foreign Operations, and Related Programs
12. Transportation, Housing and Urban Development, and Related Agencies

By tradition, all appropriations bills are House bills. Unlike other legislation that is introduced in the House or Senate, the appropriations subcommittees in the House of Representatives actually write the spending bills based on the President's budget request, the testimony given by department and agency heads, as well as the statements of outside witnesses. Get to know the subcommittee that deals with the government agency or department that interests you. It is sometimes possible to be invited to testify for five minutes before a committee if days are set aside for testimony from the general public.

This does not mean that the Senate appropriations subcommittees are not at work as well. Since everyone has the figures because of the spending "caps" for discretionary spending, the Senate also holds hearings, calls in witnesses, and often proceeds with markup and debate on its version of appropriations before the House has passed its appropriations bills. Conference committees, which meet for the most part in September, resolve the differences between the two houses so that only one final act is sent to the President for his signature.

Because of the serious efforts in recent years to cut the size of the government, the appropriations committees in both the House and the Senate actually receive their allocations (these days "ceilings") for spending as a result of the budget resolution. These allocations are known as 302(a) for the full appropriations committee and 302(b) for the subcommittees. Just a reminder, the appropriations subcommittees continue their work even in years when the budget resolution is delayed by many weeks. However, actual mark-up or writing of the bills does not take place until the 302(b) allocations are received.

By May 15th, the House Appropriations Committee may report the annual appropriations bills. The 1990 amendments to the 1974 budget timetable call for Congress to pass all appropriations bills by June 30th, leaving the remainder of the summer for conference committees to resolve differences. As was mentioned above, reality in recent years has meant that final action on many appropriations does not take place until after the start of the fiscal year. Sometimes appropriations bills are not enacted until a month or so into the following session. It should be recalled that President Clinton did not sign many of the bills for FY 1996 until April 1996, a full six months into the fiscal year.

If OMB finds that the appropriations for defense, for example, exceed the targets for a fiscal year, a sequester may occur within 15 days following passage of the legislation. Final passage of a budget should take place by October 1, the start of the new fiscal year. Final sequestration by OMB may take place within 15 days following the adjournment of Congress in the fall if the agreed-to targets have been exceeded.

The Line-Item Veto:
Past and Nullified

In 1996, Congress passed and President Clinton signed into law the "Line-Item Veto Act." It went into effect on January 1, 1997. Under the provisions of the law, the President's veto power was limited to dollar amounts specified for nonentitlement programs, such as crime fighting and dams. Entitlements,· such as Medicare and Social Security, were not included. He could also veto direct spending for programs and tax breaks for specific persons or companies.

The process operated in the following way. Congress would pass the fiscal legislation and the President would sign it as a whole, but within five calendar days excluding Sundays, he also could line out any provisions he did not like. He would then send the lined-out provisions back to Congress. If Congress did not agree with the list, it would have had 30 legislative days to pass by a simple majority vote a "joint resolution of disapproval" to protest the cancellations. If Congress disapproved, the bill of disapproval would have been sent back to the President. If he vetoed this bill, a two-thirds majority to override his veto in both houses of Congress would have been necessary. The two-thirds majority is the same ratio required by the Constitution to override a regular veto.

It should be mentioned here that there was one ruling by the Supreme Court in early summer of 1997 that the line-item veto was not, in theory, unconstitutional for it had not yet been used. This was before the President used this new power in August of 1997 to veto three items, two of a tax nature and one for spending. This new Presidential power was declared unconstitutional by the Court in 1998.

The Role of Congressional Staff in the Budget Process

It should finally be pointed out that members of Congress, both the senators and the representatives, are very busy people who often do not have the time to meet with people like you. Normally, it is not a matter of arrogance or self-importance, but rather their daily schedules can be packed for 14 hours. Direct access to the lawmakers is difficult; but this is not so with congressional staff, the chief conduits of information to the elected officials in Congress.

Every committee and subcommittee on Capitol Hill has staff. Find out who the staff on the House and Senate committees are who deal with the issues that interest you. Most citizens do not realize that the people who work on Capitol Hill, both the elected and the unelected, are smart generalists whose knowledge of an issue is miles wide but only an inch deep. To be sure, there are farmers, bankers, and business people who serve in Congress. But there is no way for them to be an expert on every single subject. All of these people need good, solid, accurate information on any given subject and you could very well be the source of that information for them. To be sure, committee staff tend to have experience, knowledge, and expertise in their issue areas. Some of the National Security Committee staff in the House, for example, are retired military. But they, too, need to have information concerning the cleanup of the area around a base that has been closed and its effect on your community.

Also realize that each representative and senator also has personal staff who work in Washington as well as in the district and state offices. Those known as legislative assistants, or LAs, work a specific issue area and often serve as liaisons with the staff of the committees that their member serves on. Just about every member of Congress has an LA assigned to national security, the environment, and veterans matters. Get to know who these people are on your representative's and two senators' staffs.

The Realities of the Budget Process on Capitol Hill

Unable to complete its budget work in a timely fashion, Congress funded the government on continuing resolutions for most of the 1980s. One notable exception occurred in the wake of the 1987 stock market crash, when the 100th Congress passed a budget for FY 1989 before the new fiscal year began.

Not much deficit reduction occurred during the Bush Administration. The passage of the Omnibus Budget Reconciliation Act in August 1993, at the beginning of Bill Clinton's presidency, reduced the deficit to about $250 billion from its high of $290 billion in 1992. Even with the caps on the discretionary dollars between 1994 and 1998, set in law by the Omnibus Budget Reconciliation Act of 1993, deficits continued because many federal programs were still in place and entitlement programs had not been capped or cut.

Summary

The continuing struggle over the budget reflects a lack of national consensus on the federal government's spending priorities. Conflicts arise due to the check-and-balance nature of the government, especially concerning who wields power over the national purse, Capitol Hill or the White House.

In 2003, divided government did not exist in Washington with the Republicans in control of both the executive and legislative branches of the federal government. In most countries of the world, there would be little if any discussion on the budget because one political party has the majority. But keep in mind that Congress is a different branch of government with different powers and prerogatives.

When the Democrats took over Congress in 2007

with disagreements over spending priorities, divided government returned to Washington, DC. In 2009, the executive and legislative branches are again led by one party, this time the Democrats.

Strategies for Action with Congress

After you have talked to the federal office about the project, the next step is to talk with the staff in your representative's district office or your senators' state offices that are closest to you. These people also work for you. Remember that your tax dollars pay their salaries. Getting the elected officials and their staffs interested in your ideas and projects only increases support at both ends of Pennsylvania Avenue. Here are some tips on communicating with members of Congress and their staffs:

- Try to get to know them before you need them. It takes time and effort but developing and maintaining a reputation for honesty and credibility is the name of the game.
- Provide fair and equal treatment to all members. You want bipartisan support for your project.
- "Information is power" in the budget process. You could well be the expert regarding the need for the requested local project or program and are the best source of information.
- Let the members and their staff know the pulse of the community. There are many more of you than there are staff.

- Try to get on a witness list to testify before an appropriations subcommittee.
- Offer written statements to the committees whose jurisdiction covers your project area. Don't forget that there are both House and Senate committees.
- Whatever the idea, program, or project, emphasize that its creation or continuation will help an agency meet its strategic planning goals.
- Make sure that the information you provide is accurate. If it is wrong and you embarrass your elected official, you may become persona non grata.

5 | *Budget Execution*

When Congress finally passes all of the appropriations bills for a new fiscal year, the bureaucracy may begin to implement some of the plans that they had made based on their budget request of some 18 months before. However, in most recent years, either because Congress and the President disagreed over budget priorities or there was internal congressional dispute, the budget is often not in place by October 1, the start of the fiscal year. Even when bills are passed on time, funds may be slow to arrive at a field office or for an activity because of internal processes within an agency. When Congress fails to agree on an appropriation bill, an Omnibus Bill may be passed for a fiscal year. This bill contains the numbers funding that departments and agencies may have available for a fiscal year.

Government officials are generally required to spend no more and no less than has been appropriated, and they may use funds only for purposes specified in law. But Congress also allows the executive branch some flexibility in spending for transfer or reprogramming funds as needed.

The Government Accountability Office now has the role of tracking Antideficiency Act violations. The Antideficiency Act prohibits government officials from spending or obligating the government to spend in advance of an appropriation, unless specific authority to do so has been provided in law.

Additionally, the Act requires the President to apportion the funds available to most executive branch agencies. The President has delegated this authority to OMB, which usually apportions by time periods (usually by quarter of the fiscal year) and sometimes by activities. Agencies may request that an account be reapportioned during the year to accommodate changing circumstances. This system helps ensure that funds are available to cover operations for the entire year. Frequently, in the first quarter of a fiscal year, an agency is slow to let contracts or purchase supplies because its managers may not be certain of the funds needed for overhead to run the programs.

If changes in laws or other factors make it necessary, Congress may enact supplemental appropriations. Before the Budget Enforcement Act of 1990, such appropriations occurred frequently. With the goals of reducing the deficits and cutting funding, agencies now receive supplemental funds only in cases of emergency.

Changing circumstances may reduce the need for certain spending for which funds have been appropriated. The President may withhold appropriated funds from budget obligation only under certain limited circumstances - to provide for contingencies, to achieve savings made possible through changes in requirements or greater efficiency of operations, or as otherwise specifically provided in law. The Impoundment Control Act of 1974 specifies the procedures that must be followed if funds are withheld. Deferrals, which are temporary withholdings, take effect immediately unless overturned by an act of Congress. In 1995, a total of $17.8 billion in deferrals was reported to Congress which it overturned. Rescissions, which permanently cancel budget authority, do not take effect unless Congress passes a law rescinding them. If such a law is not passed within 45 days of continuous session, the withheld funds must be made available for spending. In total, Congress has rescinded less than one-third of the amount of funds that Presidents have proposed for rescission since enactment of the Impoundment Control Act. In 1995, the President proposed rescissions of $1.2 billion, and Congress rescinded $0.8 billion.

The federal government monitors the executive budget, your tax dollars, through agency program managers and budget officials as well as the Inspectors General, IGs, who report to the agency head. Others within government who monitor the spending of the dollars include the Office of Management and Budget, congressional committees, and the General Accounting Office, an auditing arm of Congress. Such oversight strives to ensure that agencies comply with legal limits on spending, and that they use budget authority only for the purposes intended. This review also is designed to see that programs are operating consistently with legal requirements and existing policy, and finally to ensure that programs are well managed and achieving the intended results.

The government has paid more attention to good management through the work of Vice President Gore's National Performance Review and implementation of the 1993 Government Performance and Results Act (GPRA). This law is designed to improve government programs by using better measurements of their performance in order to evaluate their effectiveness. (See Appendix D for GPRA terms.)

6 | *Deficits and the Debt*

M ost citizens have heard a great deal about the federal budget deficit and debt in recent years, primarily because both exploded in size in the 1980s. Simply put, a deficit occurs when spending exceeds revenues in any year - just as a surplus occurs when revenues exceed spending. Generally, to finance our deficits, the Treasury borrows money. The debt is the sum total of our deficits, minus our surpluses over the years. The deficit is not a new phenomenon; the federal government incurred its first in 1792, and it generated 69 annual deficits between 1900 and 1996.

For most of the nation's history, deficits were the result of either wars or recessions. Wars necessitated major increases in military spending, while recessions reduced federal tax revenues from businesses and individuals. The federal government generated deficits during the War of 1812, the recession of 1837, the Civil War, the depression of the 1890s, and World War I. Once a war ended or the economy began to grow, the government followed its deficits with budget surpluses, with which it paid down the debt.

Deficits returned in 1931 and remained for the rest of the decade due to the Great Depression and the spending associated with President Franklin D. Roosevelt's New Deal programs. Then, World War II forced the country to spend unprecedented amounts on defense and incur unprecedented deficits. The total federal government debt actually reached an all time high of 121.7 percent of the Gross Domestic Product (GDP). Since then - with Democratic and Republican presidents, Democratic and Republican congresses - the federal government balanced its books only 11 times, most recently in 2000, the final year of Bill Clinton's presidency. The Clinton Administration, along with the GOP Republican-balancing Congress of the late 1990s, brought the debt down to 57.4 percent in 2001.

Why are deficits such a perennial problem for budget decision makers? Because spending has been growing faster than revenues. Revenues have stayed relatively constant, at around 17 to 19 percent of the Gross Domestic Product (GDP) since the 1960s. In that time, however, outlays have grown from about 17 percent of GDP in 1965 to up to nearly 24 percent in 1983, before falling to 23.6% percent today. Much of the spending growth has come in Social Security, Medicare, Medicaid, and interest payments.

Why the Deficit Is a Problem

The United States is not alone in struggling with

budget deficits. Our nation has a good record when compared to the recent economic history of six other major developed economies. You may ask, if budget deficits occur so frequently, here and abroad, should we worry about them?

The short answer is, yes. The deficit forces the government to borrow money in the private capital markets. That borrowing competes with (1) borrowing by businesses that want to build factories and machines that make workers more productive and raise incomes, and (2) borrowing by families who hope to buy new homes, cars, and other goods. The competition for funds tends to produce higher interests rates.

Deficits increase the federal debt and, with it, the government's obligation to pay interest. The more it must pay in interest, the less it has available to spend on education, law enforcement, and other important services, or the more it must collect in taxes - forever after. Today, the federal government is spending 6 percent of its budget to pay interest.

The federal interest burden grew substantially in the 1980s, both in actual dollars and as a percentage of federal income tax revenues. By 1998, net interest spending was nearly as much as the government spent on national defense. In the end, the deficit is a decision about the future of the country. It is possible to provide a solid foundation for future generations, just as parents try to do within a family by limiting the amount of debt that they pass on. Or through fiscal irresponsibility, large deficits and debt for future generations can also be created.

The budget submission for FY 2011 contained $251 billion for interest on the debt, greater than funding for the Departments of Education, Veterans, and Homeland Security combined.

Deficits and Debt

If the government incurs a deficit, it must borrow from the public. Federal borrowing involves the sale to the public of notes and bonds of varying sizes and time periods. The cumulative amount of borrowing from the public, that is, the debt held by the public - is the most important measure of federal debt because it is what the government has borrowed in the private markets over the years, and it determines how much the government pays in interest to the public.

Debt held by the public was $3.7 trillion at the end of 1996, the net effect of deficits and surpluses over the last 200 years. Fifteen years later, at the beginning of 2011, the debt totals over $13 trillion. Debt held by the public does not include debt the government owes itself - the total of all trust fund surpluses and deficits over the years, like Social Security surpluses, that the law says must be invested in federal securities. The sum total of debt held by the public and debt the government owes itself is called Gross Federal Debt.

Another measure of federal debt is debt subject to

legal limit, set by Congress, which is similar to Gross Federal Debt. When the government reaches the limits, it loses its authority to borrow more in order to finance its spending. Then Congress must enact a law that the President must sign to increase the limit.

The federal government operated in surplus from 1998 to 2001. The recession of 2001 along with the stock market crash, the terrorist attacks, and the tax cuts proposed by President George W. Bush and passed by Congress in 2001and 2001, and the wars in Iraq and Afghanistan have all contributed to the return to deficits.

It should be noted that the $5.6 trillion projected ten-year surplus that the George W. Bush administration inherited when it took office has been converted, under realistic estimates into an annual deficit of more than $1trillionfor a number of years. This represents a swing of $8.8 trillion in the wrong direction - the largest fiscal deterioration in American history.

In 2008 the American people elected Barack Obama the 44th President of the United States. He inherited serious economic and fiscal crises not known in this country since the 1930s. The combination of George W. Bush's tax cuts along with Congressional spending, the wars in Iraq and Afghanistan, the recession, and the extension of the Bush tax cuts in 2010 for two years have pushed the debt up to more than 75 percent of the GDP for FY 2011.

On February 14, 2011, President Barak Obama submitted his budget request for FY 2012. It contained an estimated deficit of $1.1 trillion. On February 13, 2012, President Obama submitted a budget request for FY 2013 with an estimated deficit of $800 billion. How will a pattern of frugality follow for the American government to get its fiscal house in order?

G | Glossary

accrual accounting A system of accounting in which revenues are recorded when earned and outlays are recorded when goods are received or services performed, even though the actual receipt of revenues and payment for goods or services may occur, in whole or in part, at a different time. Compare with cash accounting.

aggregate demand Total purchases of a country's output of goods and services by consumers, businesses, government, and foreigners during a give period. (BEA) Compare with forward funding and obligation delay.

appropriations An act of Congress that permits federal agencies to incur obligations and to make payments out of the Treasury for specified purposes. An appropriations act is the most common means of providing budget authority.

baseline A benchmark for measuring the budgetary effects of proposed changes in federal revenues or spending. For purposes of the Deficit Control Act, the baseline is the projection of current-year levels of new budget authority, outlays, revenues, and the surplus or deficit into the budget year and out-years based on current laws and policies, calculated in conformance with the rules set forth in section 257 of that act. See fiscal year.

budget authority The authority Congress gives to government agencies, permitting them to enter into obligations that will result in immediate future spending.

Forms of Budget Authority

direct spending More commonly called mandatory spending, it is a category of outlays (the disbursement of funds) from budget authority provided in law other than appropriations acts; entitlement authority and the budget authority for the Food Stamp program are examples.

discretionary appropriations A category of budget authority that comprises budget dollars (except those provided in direct-spending programs) provided in appropriations acts.

budget baseline Projected federal spending, revenue, and deficit levels based on the assumption that current policies will continue unchanged for the upcoming fiscal year.

budget deficit The amount by which the government's total outlays exceed total revenues for a given fiscal year.

Budget Enforcement Act of 1990 (BEA) The law that was designed to limit discretionary spending while ensuring that any new entitlement program or tax cut did not make the deficit worse. It set annual limits on total discretionary spending and created "pay-as-you-go" rules for any changes in entitlement and taxes.

budget function One of the 20 broad categories into which budgetary resources are grouped sot hat all budget authority and outlays can be presented according to the national interests being addressed. There are 17 broad budget function, including national defense, international affairs, energy, agriculture, health, income security, and general government. Three other functions - net interest, allowances, and undistributed offsetting receipts - are included to complete the budget. See net interest and offsetting receipts.

budget resolution A concurrent resolution, a legislative vehicle that must pass both houses of Congress, must be passed by both Houses of Congress setting forth, reaffirming, or revising the congressional budget for the U.S. Government for a fiscal year. A budget resolution is a concurrent resolution of Congress. Concurrent resolutions do not require a presidential signature because they are not laws. Budget resolutions do not need to be laws because they are a legislative device for the Congress to regulate itself as it works on spending and revenue bills.

budgetary resources All sources of authority provided to federal agencies permitting them to incur financial obligations, including new budget authority, unobligated balances, direct spending authority, and obligation limitations.

cap A legal limit on total annual discretionary spending.

cash accounting A system of accounting in which revenues are recorded when actually received and outlays are recorded when payment is made.

civilian unemployment rate Unemployment as a percentage of the civilian labor force - that is, the labor force excluding armed forces personnel.

consumer price index An index of the cost of living commonly used to measure inflation. The Bureau of Labor Statistics publishes the CPI-U, an index of consumer prices based on the typical market basket of goods and services consumed by all urban consumers during a base period, and the CPI-W, an index of consumer prices based on the typical market basket of goods and services consumed by urban wage earners and clerical workers during a base period.

continuing resolution Appropriations legislation enacted by Congress to provide temporary budget authority for federal agencies to keep them in operation when their regular appropriations bill has not been acted by the start of the fiscal year. A continuing resolution is a joint resolution, a resolution that must pass both houses of Congress and be signed by the President, which has the same legal status as a bill.

credit authority Authority to incur direct loan obligations or to incur primary loan guarantee commitments. Under the Budget Act, new credit authority must be approved in advance in an appropriations act.

credit crunch A sudden reduction in the availability of loans and other types of credit from banks and capital markets as given interest rates. The reduced availability of credit can result from many factors, including an increased perception of risk on the part of lenders, an imposition of credit controls, or a sharp restriction of the money supply.

crosswalk Sometimes used in reference to allocations made pursuant to Section 302 (and Section 602) of the Congressional Budget Act of 1974, in which the amounts set forth in a budget resolution are converted to amounts under congressional committee jurisdictions. The term "crosswalk" also may refer generally to the conversion of budgetary amounts from one classification of spending to another, such as between appropriation accounts and authorizing legislation or between budget functional structure and the congressional committee spending jurisdictions.

current services budget A section of the President's budget, required by the Budget Act, that sets forth the level of spending or taxes that would occur if existing programs and policies were continued unchanged through the fiscal year and beyond, with all programs adjusted for inflation so that existing levels of activity are maintained.

excise taxes Excise taxes apply to various products, including alcohol, tobacco, transportation fuels, and telephone service.

deficit   The amount by which the government's total budget outlays exceeds its total receipts for a fiscal year.

discretionary spending   A category of spending (budget authority and outlays) subject to the annual appropriations process.

entitlement Programs that are governed by legislation in a way that legally obligates the federal government to make specific payments to qualified recipients. Payments to persons under the Social Security, Medicare, and veteran's pensions programs are considered to be entitlements.

federal debt The gross federal debt is divided into two categories: debt held by the public, and debt the government owes itself. Another category is debt subject to legal limit.

Forms of Federal Debt

debt held by the public The total of all federal deficits, minus surpluses, over the years. This is the cumulative amount of money the federal government has borrowed from the public, through the sale of notes and bonds of varying sizes and time periods.

debt the government owes itself The total of all trust fund surpluses over the years, like the Social Security surpluses, that the law says must be invested in federal securities.

debt service Payment of scheduled interest obligations on outstanding debt. As used in CBO's Budget and Economic Outlook, debt service refers to a change in interest payments resulting from a change in estimates of the surplus or deficit.

debt subject to legal limit Roughly the same as gross federal debt, it is the maximum amount of federal securities that may be legally outstanding at any time. When the limit is reached, the President and Congress must enact a law to increase it.

depreciation Decline in the value of a currency, financial asset, or capital good. When applied to a capital good, depreciation usually refers to loss of value because of obsolescence, wear, or destruction (as by fire or flood). Book depreciation (also known as tax depreciation) is the depreciation that the tax code allows businesses to deduct when they calculate their taxable profits. It is typically faster than economic depreciation, which represents the actual decline in the value of the asset. Both measures of depreciation appear as part of the national income and product accounts.

direct spending Synonymous with mandatory spending. Direct spending is budget authority provided in laws other than appropriation acts. For purposes of the Deficit Control Act, it is also defined as including entitlement authority and the Food Stamp program.

disposable personal income The income that individuals receive, including transfer payments, minus the personal taxes and fees that they pay to governments.

domestic demand Total purchases of goods and services, regardless of origin, by U.S. consumers, businesses, and government during a given period. Domestic demand equals gross domestic product minus net exports.

entitlement A legal obligation on the federal government to make payments to a person, business, or unit of government that meets the criteria set in law. The Congress generally controls entitlement programs by setting eligibility criteria and benefit or payment rules - not by providing budget authority in an appropriation act. The source of funding to liquidate the obligation may be provided in either the authorization act that created the entitlement or a subsequent appropriation act. The best-known entitlements are the major benefit programs, such as Social Security and Medicare.

federal funds Part of the budgeting and accounting structure of the federal government. Federal funds are all funds that make up the federal budget except those classified by law as trust funds. Federal funds include several types of funds, one of which is the general fund.

federal funds rate The interest rate that financial institution charge each other for overnight loans of their monetary reserves. A rise in the federal funds rate (compared with other short-terms interest rates) suggests a tightening of the monetary policy, whereas a fall suggests an easing.

fiscal year A yearly accounting period. The federal government's fiscal year begins October 1 and ends September 30. Fiscal years are designated by the calendar years in which they end - for example, fiscal year 2004 will begin October 1, 2003 and end September 30, 2004. The budget year is the fiscal year for which the budget is being considered. In relation to a session of Congress, it is the fiscal year that starts on October 1 of the calendar year in which that session of Congress begins. An out-year is a fiscal year following the budget year. The current year is the fiscal year in progress.

functional classification A system of classifying budget resources by major purpose so that budget authority, outlays, and credit activities can be related in terms of the national needs being addressed (for example, national defense or health) regardless of the agency administering the program. There are currently 20 functions. A function may be divided into two or more subfunctions depending on the complexity of the national need addressed by that function.

general fund One type of federal funds whose receipt account is credited with federal revenues and offsetting receipts no earmarked by law for a specific purpose and whose expenditure account records amounts provided in appropriation acts or other laws for the general support of the federal government.

Gross Domestic Product (GDP) The standard measurement of the size of the economy. It is the total production of goods and services within the United States.

impoundment A generic term referring to any action or inaction by an officer or employee of the U.S. government that precludes the obligation or expenditure of budget authority in the manner intended by Congress.

line-item veto Delegates to the President the authority to cancel certain dollar amounts of discretionary budget authority provided by appropriations, new direct spending authority, and limited tax benefits.

mandatory spending Refers to spending for programs the level of which is governed by formulas or criteria set forth in authorizing legislation rather than by appropriations. Examples of mandatory spending include: Social Security, Medicare, veterans' pensions, rehabilitation services, members' pay, judges' pay, and the payment of interest on the public debt. Many of these programs are considered entitlement.

markup Meetings where congressional committees work on the language of bills or resolutions. At Budget Committee markups, the House and Senate Budget Committees work on the language and numbers contained in budget resolutions and legislation affecting the congressional budget process.

obligation limitation Legislation that reduces existing authority to incur obligations.

off-budget Those federal entities whose budget authority, outlays, and receipts have been excluded from budget totals under provisions of the law. At present, off-budget entities include the Social Security trust funds and the Postal Service.

outlays Disbursements by the Federal Treasury in the form of checks or cash. Outlays flow in part from budget authority granted in prior years and in part from budget authority provided for the year in which the disbursements occur.

pay-as-you-go Set forth by the BEA, the term refers to requirements that new spending proposals on entitlements or tax cuts must be offset by cuts in other entitlements or by other tax increases, to ensure that the deficit does not rise.

revenues Collections from the public arising from the government's sovereign power to tax. Revenues include individual and corporate income taxes, social insurance taxes (such as Social Security payroll taxes), excise taxes, estate and gift taxes, and customs duties.

reconciliation process A process by which Congress includes in a budget resolution instructions to specific committees that direct them to report legislation that changes existing laws, usually for the purpose of decreasing spending or increasing revenues by a specified amount by a certain date. The legislation may also contain an increase in the debt limit. The reported legislation is then considered as a single "reconciliation bill under expedited procedures."

rescission of budget authority Cancellation of budget authority previously provided by Congress. The Impoundment Control Act of 1974 specifies that the President may propose to Congress that funds be rescinded. If both houses of Congress have not approved a rescission proposal (by passing legislation) within 45 days continuous session, any funds being withheld must be made available for obligation.

sequester Pursuant to Gramm-Rudman-Hollings, a presidential spending reduction order that occurs by reducing defense and nondefense spending by uniform percentages.

social insurance payroll taxes This tax category includes Social Security taxes, Medicare taxes, unemployment insurance taxes, and federal employee retirement payments.

supplemental appropriation An act appropriating funds in addition to those in the 13 regular annual appropriations acts. Supplemental appropriations provide additional budget authority beyond the original estimates for programs or activities (including new programs authorized after the date of the original appropriations act) in cases where the need for funds is too urgent to be postponed until enactment of the next regular appropriations bill.

trust funds Government funds that are designated by law as trust funds (regardless of any other meaning of that term). Trust funds display the revenues, offsetting receipts or offsetting collections, and outlays that result from implementation of the law that designated the fund as a trust fund. The federal government has more than 200 trust funds. The largest and best known finance major benefit programs (including Social Security and Medicare) and infrastructure spending (the Highway and the Airport and Airway Trust Fund).

unobligated balances The portion of budget authority that has not yet been obligated. When budget authority is provided for one fiscal year, any unobligated balances at the end of that year expire and are no longer available for obligation. When budget authority is provided for a specific number of years, any unobligated balances are carried forward and are available for obligation during the years specified. When budget authority is provided for an unspecified number of years, the unobligated balances are carried forward indefinitely, until either they are rescinded, the purpose of which they were provided is accomplished, or no disbursements have been made for two consecutive years.

A | STRATEGIES FOR INPUT INTO THE EXECUTIVE BUDGET REQUEST

Now that we have outlined for you the budget formulation process, the players, and the time line within the executive branch, what follows are some practical tips to help you, the citizen, access the process.

- Get into the field office of a federal agency and talk with the local federal officials about their programs that interest you.
- Talk to the budget officer to learn the funding levels for the current fiscal year to make a plan for future dollars.
- Show the officials that your idea or program plan will help meet the needs for the agency's overall strategic plan.
- Provide support for the idea that will be convincing to top agency management and the budget office.
- Provide information in a way that may convince OMB as well.

B | STRATEGIES FOR ACTION WITH CONGRESS

After you have talked to the federal office about the project, the next step is to talk with the staff in your representative's district office or your senators' state offices that are closet to you. These people also work for you. Remember that your tax dollars pay their salaries. Getting the elected officials and their staffs interested in your ideas and projects only increases support at both ends of Pennsylvania Avenue. Here are some tips on communicating with members of Congress and their staffs:

- Try to get to know them before you need them. It takes time and effort but developing and maintaining a reputation for honesty and credibility is the name of the game.
- Provide fair and equal treatment to all members. You want bipartisan support for your project.
- "Information is power" in the budget process. You could well be the expert regarding the need for the requested local project or program and are the best source of information.
- Let the members and their staff know the pulse of the community. There are many more of you

than there are staff.

- Try to get on a witness list to testify before an appropriations subcommittee.
- Offer written statements to the committees whose jurisdiction covers your project area. Don't forget that there are both House and Senate committees.
- Whatever the idea, program, or project, emphasize that its creation or continuation will help an agency meet its strategic planning goals.
- Make sure that the information you provide is accurate. If it is wrong and you embarrass your elected official, you can become persona non grata.

C | GOVERNMENT PERFORMANCE AND RESULTS ACT *(GPRA)*

general goal A general goal is an elaboration of the mission statement, developing with greater specificity how an agency will carry out its mission. The goal may have a programmatic, policy, or management nature. It is expressed in a manner that allows a future assessment to be made of whether the goal was or is being achieved.

general objective A general objective is often synonymous with a general goal. In a strategic plan, an objective may complement a general goal whose achievement cannot be directly measured. The assessment is made on the objective rather than the general goal. Objectives may also be characterized as being particularly focused on the conduct of basic agency functions and operations (e.g., computer capacity, staff training and skills) that support the conduct of programs and activities.

outcome goal A description of the intended result, effect, or consequence that will occur from carrying out a program or activity.

output goal A description of the level of activity or effort that will be produced or provided over a period of time or by a specified date, including a description of the characteristics and attributes (e.g., timeliness) established as standards in the course of conducting the activity or effort.

performance goal A target level of performance expressed as a tangible, measurable objective, against which actual achievement can be compared, including a goal expressed as a quantitative standard, value, or rate.

performance indicator A particular value or characteristic used to measure output or outcome.

program activity A specific activity or project as listed in the program and financing schedules of the annual budget of the U.S. government.

program evaluation An assessment, through objective measurement and systematic analysis, of the manner and extent to which federal programs achieve intended objectives.

D | *Key Websites*

Executive Branch

The White House
whitehouse.gov

Department of Agriculture
usda.gov

Department of Commerce
doc.gov

Department of Defense
defenselink.mil

Department of Education
ed.gov

Department of Energy
energy.gov

Department of Health and Human Services
hhs.gov

Department of Housing and Urban Development
hud.gov

Department of Interior
doi.gov

Department of Justice
usdoj.gov

Department of Labor
dol.gov

Department of State
state.gov

Department of Transportation
dot.gov

Department of the Treasury
ustreas.gov

Department of Veterans' Affairs
va.gov

Legislative Branch

United States Senate
senate.gov

Senate Appropriations Committee
appropriations.senate.gov

Senate Budget Committee
budget.senate.gov

Senate Finance Committee
finance.senate.gov

United States House of Representatives
house.gov

House Appropriations Committee
appropriations.house.gov

House Budget Committee
budget.house.gov

House Ways and Means Committee
waysandmeans.house.gov

General Accounting Office
gao.gov

Government Printing Office
gpo.gov

Library of Congress
thomas.loc.gov

American Recovery and Reinvestment Act
recovery.gov

Government Printing Office
fdsys.gpo.gov

11702828R00079

Made in the USA
Charleston, SC
15 March 2012